Clarissa de Waal is a Social Anthropologist and Fellow Emerita of Newnham College, Cambridge. She is the author of *Albania: Portrait of a Country in Transition* and *Everyday Iran: A Provincial Portrait of the Islamic Republic* (both I.B.Tauris).

BEYOND THE BAILOUTS

The Anthropology and History
of the Greek Crisis

CLARISSA DE WAAL

I.B. TAURIS

LONDON · NEW YORK

This book is dedicated to the many Greeks who have helped me over the years to gain an insight into the challenges and aspirations which make up their daily lives. Warm friendships and stimulating discussions have been a pleasure which will I hope last long beyond the bailouts. My daughter Issa, supportive reader and constructive critic, has been an invaluable source of encouragement.

Published in 2018 by
I.B.Tauris & Co. Ltd
London • New York
www.ibtauris.com

International Library of Economics 10

ISBN: 978 1 78831 259 2
eISBN: 978 1 78672 400 7
ePDF: 978 1 78673 400 6

A full CIP record for this book is available from the British Library
A full CIP record is available from the Library of Congress

Library of Congress Catalog Card Number: available

Typeset in Garamond Three by OKS Prepress Services, Chennai, India
Printed and bound by CPI Group (UK) Ltd, Croydon, CR0 4YY

CONTENTS

CONTENTS

INTRODUCTION

From 2010, 'the crisis' – 'η κρισή' – was the phrase on everyone's lips and the central media topic in Greece. Abroad interest was intense largely thanks to the cliff-hanger factor: would Greece be forced to leave the euro and go back to the drachma? Could leaving the euro actually be better for Greeks? Might there be a domino effect such that the whole European Union (EU) project was endangered? Before each new bailout there was more suspense, another θριλερ – 'thriller' – as the television anchors put it: will we get it, won't we get it? The threatened exit, now dubbed Grexit, led to a division of opinion abroad between those who saw the Greeks as profligate spendthrifts and those who believed that the European Commission, the European Central Bank and the International Monetary Fund (IMF) – the troika – were destroying the economy by imposing such a harsh programme of austerity. It also gave rise to a much wider debate concerning the character of the EU: is it dysfunctional, undemocratic or beyond reform? In 2015 the recently elected left-wing Syriza government called a referendum in which the majority voted against the troika-proposed austerity measures but at the same time to stay with the euro, a result that threatened to derail the whole European project and/or to be the end of Alexis Tsipras, leader of the Syriza party. Neither of these outcomes came to pass and a third bailout was negotiated. Greeks got poorer and poorer, the welfare system became increasingly broken and the troika's interventions were seen as counterproductive, turning Greece into a 'debt colony', said some. One of the most outstanding characteristics of the crisis has been its longevity, with Greece repeatedly near collapse, sometimes so close to the edge of the cliff that Grexit seemed inevitable, but each time pulling back just before it was too late.

Greece's place in Western culture as the cradle of civilisation undoubtedly contributed to interest abroad; another small country whose economy was barely two per cent of the EU's might have attracted less attention. Likewise, geographically and geopolitically its proximity to the rest of the Balkans and to Turkey endows it with strategic significance. We are seeing a geographical importance or vulnerability during the refugee crisis, where this struggling economy is failing to cope with thousands of refugees.

Asked over the years what led to the crisis, Greeks often take much of the blame for themselves while adding that the real problems began in the 1980s when Andreas Papandreou and his Pasok party were in power. Some see leaving the drachma for the euro as the core mistake; some believe that the country's plight is the result of a German plot to buy up Greece. Many trace the problems to Ottoman taxation methods while a minority lays the blame on the Byzantines. The causes and effects of economic breakdown have been the subject of illuminating analysis by economists and investigative journalists. This book's attempt to identify some initial causes takes a different methodological approach in that I draw on anthropological research extending from the 1980s to the crisis period to substantiate my thesis that the nineteenth-century Greek diaspora activities were core contributors to Greece's economic problems.

How did the crisis start and why does it go on and on?

To begin to answer these questions it is enlightening to go back to the period shortly after the War of Independence (1821–32) when the Greek diaspora numbered about three million, compared to the 700,000–800,000 mainly rural inhabitants inside Greece.[1] As a first step towards Hellenising Greece following centuries of Ottoman rule, diaspora members started to introduce an extensive education system throughout rural Greece. This became a valuable resource from which to draw educated young men to work in diaspora communities abroad. When the diaspora, inspired by newly aroused nationalist sentiment, set about re-establishing Athens as the capital and centre of Hellenism, the existence of substantial numbers of educated villagers was opportune. The new capital became the centre of a huge administration attracting large numbers of rural migrants who, it is important to note, differed radically from the marginalised landless masses escaping rural misery in Spain, Italy or South America. Feudal estates were the exception in Greece except in a few northern areas, and most farming was in the hands of small owner-cultivators. These Greek migrants were mostly better-off educated villagers whose object was to find work in the public sector, an aim that they were able to realise through clientelist links with government representatives. Although the city's population increased rapidly, it is significant that there were few of the usual signs of proletarianisation, unemployment or slum settlements associated with fast-growing cities. On the contrary, migrants' arrival in Athens was followed by their easy absorption into the urban middle class. There were very few opportunities for secondary sector workers, apart from shipbuilding in Piraeus, since Athens itself had no productive base. The diaspora, rather than investing their ample capital in manufacturing and industry, chose to finance this huge administration from their commercial enterprises outside Greece. This reluctance to invest in a productive base to sustain the growing city had long-term social, economic and political consequences. On the socio-economic front a move to Athens became identified by the rural population with a rise in social status, transforming a practical aspiration for a state sector city job into an ideology that saw this move as the key to social prestige. Intrinsic to this ideology was a repudiation of village life as backward, only for those too stupid to leave it. Clientelist interests (jobs for votes) fostered this ideology of 'urban aspiration', with negative effects on the administration, which became far larger than necessary and increasingly stretched economically. Indeed the Greek government was already heavily indebted to those foreign powers whose help they had had to invoke when they found that they could not win the War of Independence without outside support. Nor could diaspora funds permanently sustain an ever-expanding public sector.

Greece's geopolitical position

Creditors rarely lend disinterestedly and Britain's primary motive in the case of the very large sums lent to the Greek government in 1824 and 1825 was the wish to prevent Russian and Egyptian territorial expansion. No doubt, as some have argued, the profits to be earned from the loan were an additional draw.[2] Greece's subsequent political dependency despite winning independence from Ottoman rule was confirmed when in 1832 the allied powers agreed to install the 17-year-old Otho of Bavaria as king of Greece. Bavarian regents ruled for him until he came of age while the allied powers oversaw his government. At the same time, thanks to its geopolitical importance, Greece was able to become a serial borrower despite repeated defaults and bankruptcies. Foreign powers' fear of different forces, whether Russian, German or Communist depending on the period, could be taken advantage of repeatedly.

On the economic front it is revealing to look more closely at these defaults and bankruptcies as explored by two economists, Carmen Reinhart and Christoph Trebesch, in a working paper 'The Pitfalls of External Dependence: Greece, 1829–2015'. The economic–financial point they are making goes beyond the Greek situation, centring on the difference between the effects on a country of raising loans privately as opposed to borrowing from foreign governments. In the context of this book, their argument is particularly pertinent as they point out that the events since 2010 are neither new nor unique in Greek history; one clue as to why the crisis goes on and on. They see Greek history as a narrative of debt, default and external dependence:

> Two centuries of Greek debt crises highlight the pitfalls of relying on external financing. Since its independence in 1829, the Greek government has defaulted four times on its external creditors – with striking historical parallels. Each crisis is preceded by a period of heavy borrowing from foreign private creditors. As repayment difficulties arise, foreign governments step in, help to repay the private creditors, and demand budget cuts and adjustment programs as a condition for the official bailout loans. Political interference from abroad mounts and a prolonged episode of debt overhang and financial autarky follows. We conclude that these cycles of external debt and dependence are a perennial theme of Greek history, as well as in other countries that have been 'addicted' to foreign savings.[3]

The lesson as seen in the twenty-first century is that relying heavily on external borrowing leads to oppressive intervention from abroad; intervention that critically prioritises repayment of the bailout loans over aiding a country's economic recovery. The cyclical character of Greece's recurrent problems with its creditors is echoed in the similarity of the reforms demanded each time. In 1990 the *Financial Times*[4] noted that the European Commission was demanding that Greece make a ten per cent cut in public sector staffing by 1993 involving the loss of at least 65,000 jobs. The introduction of new taxes and new laws designed to reduce the enormously high level of tax evasion was similarly demanded. In 2010 and 2011 when the Greek government was seeking massive loans, the lenders – the troika – made the bailout conditional on the implementation of a detailed and extensive programme of fiscal and structural austerity measures. These included tax increases, spending cuts, privatisation of state-controlled corporations, selling-off of state assets, slashing of salaries, reduction of pensions and the dismissal initially of 30,000 public sector workers, the first of 150,000 to be dismissed by 2016. To avoid a Greek default the troika agreed in November 2012 to a second bailout with more austerity measures attached including a further cut to the healthcare system of €2 billion. Compare these to the measures imposed in 1843 (as recorded by Eric Toussaint adapted from Takis Katsimardos):[5]

In June 1843, unable to afford the annual tranche of interest payments on the 1833 loan, Greece was forced to default. Faced with threats from the creditors, the government undertook to apply a brutal austerity programme to enable them to keep on servicing their debt. Greece then entered a phase of 'extreme' austerity. Sources of the time report scenes of mass hardship, in town and country. In the capital, penniless citizens stopped paying their taxes to the point where there were no candidates for the once coveted post of tax-collector, previously attributed by auction! Obviously it was impossible to collect money for debt servicing in a country where the majority of the population was living in utter deprivation. Yet the creditors continued to demand the debt payments. The situation led to a conference being held in London on Greek debt where the representatives of the Troika redacted a statement condemning Greece (June 1843). The statement declared that Greece had failed to fulfil her obligations. The three ambassadors gave the government 15 days to make even more drastic cuts in public spending to raise the sum of about 4 million GDR. The cuts that the government had initially planned would only have levied 1 million GDR. After a month of discussions, a memorandum protocol was drawn up by the ambassadors and the Greek government. The agreement was ratified on 2 September, giving rise to a storm of protest. The next day was the start of the 3 September 1843 Revolution, which was to result in a new Constitution that was still far from democratic. The main measures taken by the Greek government in 1843 in application of the Memorandum of that time included:

1. Laying off one third of civil servants and reducing the salaries of those remaining by 15–20%;
2. Suspension of retirement pension payments;
3. Considerable reduction of military spending;
4. Payment by all producers of an advance on tax called a 'tithe', corresponding to a tenth of the value of everything produced;
5. Increases in customs duties and stamp duties;
6. Laying off all civil servants in the National Printers, forest wardens and most university professors (all but 26!);
7. Closure of all state health services;
8. All State civil engineers laid off and all public works projects halted;
9. Cancellation of all diplomatic missions abroad;
10. Legalization of all illegal constructions and illegally appropriated land belonging to the state, upon payment of a fine;
11. Regularization of all pending tax fraud cases (to the value of 5 million GDR) on payment of a modest sum.

Furthermore, in line with the terms of the 'Memorandum', the ambassadors of the Troika countries of that time were present at all cabinet meetings where the measures were validated, and were sent detailed reports every month concerning their implementation and the monies collected.

This nineteenth-century social and economic background makes up the first section of the book, which explores the circumstances leading to the inception of an ideology that it is argued has been a significant contributor to Greece's problematic development. The next sections of the book are based on analysis following two extensive periods of ethnographic research.

The ethnography

The first research project was carried out in southern Greece in the 1980s and early 1990s. Its object was to determine whether in view of an improving economic situation in the provinces there would be a change in attitude towards village-based activities and a rise in exploitation of local opportunities; perhaps even a return flow from Athens. Although I remained in close touch with my Greek fieldwork area while carrying out research in Albania and later in Iran, I did not resume recording fieldwork observations on Greece until 2008. At the time of the first twenty-first-century bailout in 2010 I decided to make the 'crisis' and its causes the subject of this book. This involved fieldwork in Athens as well as in the provincial area studied earlier.

Starting in the mid-1980s my research encompassed two areas either side of the Spartan valley. Following the ravages to the countryside of World War II and the Civil War (1946–9) there had been a huge rural exodus mainly to transatlantic destinations, but also to Germany (from northern Greece) and to Athens. In common with the predominant trend throughout Greece and with those villages studied in earlier ethnographies, my first fieldwork area had experienced a very high level of out-migration. By the 1980s, however, the area had recovered from earlier setbacks and was relatively prosperous with fertile agricultural land and an important though under-valued Byzantine site. Many villagers' incomes were boosted by remittances from émigrés or foreign pensions in the case of returnees – about a third of the inhabitants. When I began fieldwork in the mid-1980s the new Socialist government's policy of decentralisation, whose stated goal was the demographic and economic reconstruction of the countryside, was having a positive impact. Likewise European Economic Community (EEC) subsidies were strengthening the agricultural sector. Yet the conviction that to be a success one must have a public sector job in the capital persisted despite very good economic reasons for avoiding it. Athens was experiencing growing unemployment, severe air pollution and higher commodity prices. But village life was despised and one's children must be educated out of it. The result over the years was economic stagnation and ultimately depopulation.

The discovery that villages impervious to this urban aspiring ideology were to be found across the Spartan valley led me to extend my research to what turned out to be an actively productive area. It was on a similar level in terms of economic potential but differed in that it had experienced much lower emigration and was fully utilising local opportunities. This was a conundrum in that it completely departed from the predominant trend. Further research indicated that earlier relations of production had played a significant role since these had been more favourable to villagers, resulting in the much lower level of out-migration. The ideology of aspiration to work in the public sector, albeit pervasive, was not after all subscribed to across the board in Greece.

One of the most striking findings from several years of research in these areas was the conservatism of the first area and the modernity of the second; 'modernity' in the sense of responsiveness to change, experimentation, openness to new ideas. The first area's inhabitants aspired to be as urban as possible in work and appearance. They modelled their behaviour on what they believed to define the modern, that is, the urban, as represented by Athens, a world as they saw it away from manual work and dirt and backwardness. Anyone who tried to introduce new ideas in these villages was resented as a threat socially and economically, and where possible thwarted. New ideas ranged from opening a restaurant to setting up a tourist camping site to embarking on a farming career. This last was the greatest affront since for a successful returnee to choose to invest in an occupation spurned locally as demeaning undermined established priorities.

When some young villagers, educated in Athens, responding to negative developments in the capital, did return to live in the village they soon encountered resistance to their projected reforms from an old guard unwilling to see changes introduced that challenged the status quo. Despite brave efforts initially, the young eventually left the village, with adverse effects on village productivity. Comparing these developments with the dynamic activities of the agricultural area, I concluded that the effects of urban aspiration in the Greek context constitute a retrograde force, a promoter of economic stagnation.

Economic stagnation, the outcome of the urban aspiring majority's unproductive activities, begged the question of how long could the country's unreformed government continue to support this population without collapsing economically? A history of combating unemployment by handing out public sector jobs, a parasitic economy largely based on rentier capitalism, a very big informal sector and very high rate of tax evasion had combined to render Greece's economy ultimately unsustainable. An answer came in 2010 when Greece received its first twenty-first-century bailout. The capital, with nearly half the country's population based in greater Athens, was the first to be hit by the debt crisis. A succession of bailouts conditional on detailed and extensive reforms imposed by the lenders set in train years of increasing indebtedness, very high unemployment and ever-growing doubts that Grexit could be avoided.

Returning in 2014 from a year's fieldwork in Athens to the provinces, I found that productivity and incomes in the agriculturally active villages had continued to increase, bucking the latest trend of indebtedness and closures seen most starkly in Greek towns. While these farmers did not suffer a fall in income between 2010 and 2016, the crisis had spurred them to look even more proactively for new ways to generate income, not least because they were about to be taxed on an up-to-date basis costing them much more than in the past. By contrast, urban-aspiring villagers have largely ignored both agricultural opportunities and alternative enterprises, still preferring to move to towns and in increasing numbers to emigrate. Without systemic reform in government institutions such that bureaucracy facilitates rather than obstructs, without functioning laws to crack down on tax evasion and corrupt practices, without policies to underpin production and export, it is hard to see how Greece can move back from its long-term position at the edge of the Grexit cliff.

CHAPTER 1

ASTIFILIA AND THE ROOTS OF THE GREEK CRISIS

What is *astifilia*?

The Greek crisis has highlighted a feature of the country's development by which I had been particularly struck when doing fieldwork in southern Greece in the 1980s. This was the widespread ambition to *'piastei sto dimosio'* – to latch on to the public sector. The symbiosis between public-sector employment and entrenched political clientelism – MPs handing out state jobs in exchange for votes – has been a major factor in Greece's problematic economic development. Access to employment through clientelistic means as opposed to meritocratic criteria has contributed to the number of poorly qualified employees in an already-inflated state administration and to the over-concentration of a large unproductive middle class in the capital.

Aspiration to middle-class urban employment, preferably in the civil service or professions (doctor, lawyer), and the consequent emphasis on education, is of course historically widespread in developing countries.[1] Thus at first sight one might assume that Greek urban aspiration was related to the economic rationale underlying the rural–urban migrations characteristic of, for example, Latin American countries – the exodus of the rural poor, usually a landless proletariat, in search of employment in the cities.[2] However, examination both of the rural conditions and of migrants' situation in urban Greece clearly demonstrates a fundamental difference. As the political scientist Keith Legg noted: 'In Greece, peasants have not been forced off the land, the move to the city has been voluntary.'[3] Similarly, the sociologist Nikos Mouzelis, writing about Athens: 'there exists no huge slum-dwelling Lumpenproletariat'.[4] There has never been, he points out, an equivalent in Greece to the Turkish *gecekondu*, Brazilian favela or nineteenth-century London slum. Marginalised uneducated masses have not been part of the Greek urban scene. On the contrary, the urban population has been notable for the much greater size of the middle class as compared with the non-white-collar class. In this respect the Greek experience also diverges from that of other Mediterranean countries. The absence of latifundia in Greece (apart from the Boeotian and Thessalian plains) distinguishes it from Spain and Italy. It was exceptional in Greece to find a landless rural proletariat migrating to escape from abysmal conditions and the hardship and uncertainties of agricultural wage labour such as those observed by Hans Buechler in Spain.[5] Nor is there a parallel with the Italian situation described by William Douglass who sees the Italian rural poor as 'one of Europe's most impoverished and downtrodden rural proletariats [...] in the city the rural migrant encounters prejudice, discrimination, lack of services, poor housing, and job insecurity'.[6]

What distinguishes the Greek case is the country's unusual urban formation. Here the activities of Greece's wealthy diaspora during the Ottoman period and immediately following the War of Independence were crucial. In the nineteenth century the diaspora, 3 million-strong compared to the *c*.800,000 mainly rural inhabitants inside Greece, shifted some of their activities for the first time to Athens, where following independence from the

Ottomans they set about establishing a large state administration. This change of direction was partly a response to the diaspora's diminishing popularity abroad as ethnic consciousness in the host countries grew. It was also the result of a newly aroused cultural patriotism – Hellenism – whose aim was to re-establish Greece as the birthplace of European culture.

As a first step, an extensive education network was gradually established throughout the Greek countryside in the belief that educating the people would aid Greece's future liberation from the Ottoman yoke. Education had always been of prime importance to the diaspora, but not until the end of the eighteenth century did it become identified with the liberation of Greece. It was this access to education that enabled villagers to be recruited by members of the diaspora for service sector employment in diaspora centres abroad and subsequently for jobs in Athens. The ease with which a villager could be absorbed into the urban white-collar class led to an association between a move to Athens or a diaspora centre and a rise in social status. Eventually the ideological implications of getting a position in the *dimosio* (public service) transcended the utilitarian. Thus *astifilia* (literally 'love of the town') became an ideology; it was not, as one American anthropologist considered it, a term used by Greeks for the process of urbanisation.[7] The Greek word for urbanisation is '*astikopoiisi*', a value-free term describing a process, while *astifilia* is a value-loaded term that refers to the perceived superiority of the city as a locus of social prestige in contrast to the village, which represents backwardness.

It is illuminating to compare *astifilia* with the Italian *civiltà* as explained by the social anthropologist Sydel Silverman:

> Civiltà is an ideology about *civilisation*. Such ideologies must be defined in native terms [...] In looking at the case of Montecastello, I think it can be shown that the several elements of civiltà can be related to patterns of social behaviour that are the products of certain political and

economic conditions. In other words, I see ideology as rooted in social action and, in turn, the material basis of such action. If civiltà is an ideology about town life, then tracing its roots may expose some of the processes that have shaped town – and country – in this part of central Italy [...] Since our theory defined such areas [rural areas and small communities] as 'periphery', in relation to a center, usually in the city, we found it noteworthy that people of the periphery might claim civilisation and urbanity, cultural attributes of the center.[8]

[...] the urban phenomenon extends also to small nuclei of the hinterlands; in a real sense it has fashioned the countryside.[9]

In like vein the anthropologist Thomas Crump writes:

Italy, above all, is the country where the city comes first, where urban institutions permeate and dominate the countryside, which is seen as a sort of rural retreat from the city [...] The sophistication of urban institutions, and their *extension* [my emphasis] outside the city walls, are historically the most remarkable common denominator of Italy as a whole [...] At the core of this divergence is the political structure of each area. The constitutional unification of the three tier devolution of government in Italy, through the region, the province and the commune, does give even the smallest commune an air of civic importance.[10]

These passages highlight an essential difference between *civiltà* and *astifilia*. The latter implies a rejection of the provinces as opposed to a desire to import the attributes of the town to the countryside. *Civiltà* is an ideology about the essence of town life whose qualities of civility, the urbane and the civic are *diffused* throughout the countryside. *Astifilia* is an ideology that perceives civilisation and urbanity as *incompatible* with the countryside. Moreover, the regional autonomy and decentralisation referred to by Crump is the reverse of the highly centralised political structure of nineteenth- and twentieth-century Greece.

Post-Ottoman centralisation

To understand the factors that led to this divergent development, one might start by looking at Greece after 1821 and the War of Independence, when the centralising tendencies of the Greek state increased as local oligarchies under the Ottoman state lost control over their provincial territories. The land that pre-Independence had been under the aegis of the Turkish landlords[11] was not taken over on their departure by local notables (tax collectors for the Porte, archons) who had hoped to succeed them, but by the state,[12] whose object was precisely to prevent the emergence and consolidation of a strong landowning class.[13] Hence these notables who under the Ottomans had held positions of influence, often over successive generations, were forced to look for alternative power bases. They started investing in the urban property market, in export business, in commercial shipping and usury. Crucially, in order to consolidate their changed position they attached themselves to the rapidly expanding state administration. This withdrawal of the potentially powerful from the provinces and the notables' infiltration of the state administration had long-lasting consequences for Greece's subsequent political development. Firstly, the traditional view of administrators under the Ottomans that a public post was a source of private profit to its holder rather than an instrument of public benefit transferred itself to the new state administration. Secondly, despite no longer being active in agricultural concerns, these former rural 'bigmen' used their new position as Members of Parliament to hand out favours and civil service positions in exchange for the small owner-cultivators' votes. By connecting the provincial population to the central institutions of the state through the prospect of state sector jobs in exchange for electoral support,[14] the new MPs were in a strong position to woo and retain their rural clienteles. With neither a powerful landowning class nor a provincially based professional class (doctors, lawyers, educated farmers and clergy) as found in nineteenth-century England or France to endow the countryside with social status, power and prestige became identified with the urban administration.

The shift to centralisation had a detrimental effect on Greece's provincial towns. At the beginning of the nineteenth century when Greece was still a part of the Ottoman Empire, there were three kinds of towns: commercial and administrative centres established at strategic inland communication points; commercial centres that were ports or export points; and island towns whose prosperity was based on shipping enterprises. These centres which functioned comparatively autonomously were part of a legal, economic and social network whose decentralised nature was characteristic of the Ottoman administrative system. But following the establishment of Athens as the capital of Greece the formerly autonomous towns lost their administrative functions to Athens. Meanwhile decades of fighting had terminated the manufacturing activities and exports of the commercial centres. The only towns outside Athens to thrive were Ermopoulis, a centre of shipbuilding, and Patras and Kalamata, ports for the export of currants. By the end of the nineteenth century these too declined. Sailing vessels were superseded by the steamship, and shipbuilding moved to Athens' port, Piraeus. This loss of economic dynamism and administrative autonomy in the provincial towns further strengthened the capital's dominance but not its economic dynamism.

Athens: centre of non-productivity

The rapid growth of Athens throughout the nineteenth century following Independence (Athens' population: 1800 — 10,000;

1853 – 36,000; 1870 – 60,000; 1889 – 149,000; 1896 – 180,000; 1907 – 250,000; 1920 – 453,000)[15] was in stark contrast to the decline of every other urban settlement in Greece. But while it took over all administration it took over no productive activities apart from shipbuilding, centred in Piraeus. Industry, inasmuch as it existed at all, failed even to cover the urban population's needs. It was so underdeveloped that Greece was importing both raw materials such as wood, metal and cotton (despite indigenous cotton production) and ready-made commodities from dyed cloth to furniture, to screws and nails.[16] There are various explanations for this failure to industrialise beyond shipbuilding. A major inhibiting factor may have been the inadequate material infrastructure. For instance, until 1880 the road network was only 620 kilometres and the railway network covered no more than 11 kilometres.[17] The absence of a sizeable proletariat was clearly an obstacle, and the fate of the earlier artisanal textile industries may well have been a disincentive. These had flourished in the north of Greece in the eighteenth century and were responsible, according to the historian Kremmidas, for 30 per cent of the gross national product of Greece until their development was cut short by the English industrial revolution.[18] But perhaps the most likely explanation for failure to industrialise was the diaspora's reluctance to invest in long-term projects; a legacy of their historical role as middlemen for whom quick profits were more expedient given the merchant's position of insecurity and often illegality under the Ottomans.

Despite being neither a manufacturing nor an industrial centre Athens was attracting huge numbers of rural migrants. The majority of these, like those to the diaspora centres, were members of better-off small cultivator families whose labour could be spared. Like those who migrated to Asia Minor, these migrants planned to establish themselves in petit-bourgeois service-sector salaried jobs: a plan based on a realistic assessment of their chances in the job market, as indicated by the low level of unemployment in Athens, where up until 1922 (the year of the Asia Minor crisis) the lack of proletarianisation was striking. In 1870 there were 31,234 salaried workers in Athens.[19] The statistics for housing demonstrate that there was no overcrowding,[20] while foreign observers' reports[21] note the absence of signs of poverty such as beggars or slum tenements. The French writer Edmond About commented on the rootlessness of Athens, its isolation from the rest of Greece, the absence of links between the city and the hinterland: no suburbs, no built-in productive functions. 'Were the government to move elsewhere, there would be nothing to retain this population.'[22]

The historian Evelpidis in his *Social and Economic History of Greece* notes that by 1880, 75 per cent of the non-agricultural active population of Greece was not directly involved in production but belonged to the service sector.[23] This included a huge public administration, a larger number of lawyers than any other European country at the time (in 1883 one per cent of the non-agricultural workforce were lawyers); 400 MPs for an electorate of under one million (cf. the UK's 650 MPs for a population of *c.*65 million in 2016); a large military staff and numerous teachers and doctors. At the same time there was no significant unemployment and the service sector was made up of the better-off stably employed bourgeoisie. In short, the state had become the largest source of employment, with civil service jobs concentrated in Athens. It has been calculated that in 1890 civil servants and their families constituted one-twelfth of Greece's population.[24] On the basis of Bickford-Smith's figures,[25] the Greek sociologist Konstantinos Tsoukalas calculates that in 1889 there were 214 civil servants for every 10,000 inhabitants, compared with 73 in England, 176 in France, 126 in Germany and 113 in the USA, despite far more developed urbanisation in those countries. It is true that in all the Balkan countries the creation of a centralised urban state preceded the development of an urban society, acquiring a much larger personnel than its functions warranted, but whereas in 1920 Yugoslavia's service sector employed 6.8 per cent of the total active population and Bulgaria 9.5 per cent, Greece employed 21.1 per cent. Most strikingly, the secondary sector in Athens was so limited that foreign workers had to be imported. For example, in the construction industry most of the workers were Bulgarian.[26]

Diaspora wealth: colonials in their own country

The question arises: how could this vast state administration and huge service sector be financed given the low level of productivity throughout this period? It is all the more an enigma in view of Greece's bankruptcy in 1893 when the allied powers had to take control over certain revenues.[27] (The resonances with the twenty-first-century debt crisis are striking.) Public loans made in the European financial market and loans from the British for the construction of a railway network do not explain how this parasitic population was maintained. The agricultural surplus was inadequate even to provide for the urban population, whose food and luxury commodities had to be imported; between 1851 and 1912, exports only covered 40–70 per cent of the value of imports, sometimes less.[28]

The answer to this enigma lies in the continuous injections of capital by the Greek diaspora. From the 1840s onwards a steady stream of Greeks from the diaspora urban centres established themselves in Athens. One factor behind this move to Athens, as noted above, was the host countries' growing ethnic consciousness and increasing resentment towards the large Greek population in their midst. At first these diaspora Greeks maintained their economic enterprises abroad, but they were now beginning to transfer their profits to Greece, where they invested them in new building projects in Athens. In fact it is calculated that by 1880 over half (59 per cent)[29] of Athens' large imposing buildings had been built by diaspora Greeks. Fortunes made outside Greece also financed numerous philanthropic works within the country such as hospitals, schools, libraries and museums, a clear indication of growing patriotic feelings on the diaspora's part.

After 1870 there was an influx of bankers and rich businessmen from diaspora centres, transferring large amounts of capital, resulting in a proliferation of banks and insurance companies. In 1876 the Stock Exchange was established and shipping companies transferred their bases to Athens. The establishment of Athens as a financial centre ensured the growth of the service sector at the same time as perpetuating the city's non-productive parasitic character. Apart from the purchase of the Lavriou mines, capital was not invested in productive under-takings. Despite the presence of more than adequate capital, there were no entrepreneurs willing to invest in industry; quick trade profits were preferred or capital was invested abroad. Yet Greece was probably the only small country with enough capital at its disposal to have developed a flourishing industry. Instead, the diaspora's exclusively merchant role in Asia Minor was reproduced within the framework of Greece, with serious consequences for its subsequent economic development. The diaspora capitalist activities were in effect much like British, French and German colonial activities in the countries of their empires, where exploitation of ores, building of railways and founding of banks similarly took place. But these Greek colonists were colonising their own country, itself a dependent subject of capitalist powers, with no capital-rich country of their own to back up these activities.[30]

The diaspora before the War of Independence

In order to understand how the state administration was able economically to expand so extensively, we need to go back and look at the diaspora activities pre-Independence. How had the large diaspora become so rich and why did it eventually shift the focus of its activities from abroad to Greece? Starting in the sixteenth century, the major European states negotiated a series of trading privileges from the Porte, which increased as the Ottoman state declined. Greek merchants were involved both in Ottoman internal trade and in commerce in the Black Sea and Adriatic. In the eighteenth century they were able to take advantage of the trade vacuum in the Mediterranean resulting from the Anglo-French wars. Their commercial dominance during Ottoman rule was further boosted by the position of the Greek Orthodox Church, which was the main link between the Sultan and his subjects. Interestingly, Greek became the language of all upwardly mobile Balkan merchants, eventually becoming the language for culture and education irrespective of the subject's ethnicity.[31] By the eighteenth century there were substantial Greek diaspora communities in Russia, the Balkans, the major European capitals, southern France (Marseilles) and Asia Minor. These communities were flourishing centres of Greek culture with schools, printing presses and churches, as well as businesses. While the Greek communities in central Europe began to decline from the beginning of the nineteenth century as Greeks became absorbed into the local upper-middle class, the diaspora centres in Asia Minor and, later on, Egypt were growing fast. Smyrna's Greek community grew from 8,000 inhabitants in 1739 to 120,000 in 1885; Constantinople's grew from 80,000 in 1800 to 500,000 in 1920; while Egypt's changed from no Greeks in 1840 to 200,000 in 1922.[32]

At the start of the nineteenth century when under a million people, mostly rural and poor, lived within Greece, the urban Greek diaspora largely concentrated in Asia Minor was at least three times as big. These Greeks (with smaller numbers of Armenians and Jews) acted as commercial and financial negotiators between the Ottoman territories and those western European countries with capital at their disposal. Being mobile, polyglot and literate (unlike most of the Turkish population), the

Greeks were able to take over banking, usury and commerce. As these commercial activities expanded they began to import personnel from Greece to staff their offices. Here the extensive schools network referred to earlier came into its own. Between 1834 and 1840, 60,000 young men, villagers from the small owner-cultivator areas, left for such jobs.[33] It is estimated that nearly one in three small owner-cultivator families had a son who left for clerical and mercantile activities in the diaspora centres.[34] Transmission of property in Greece is through partible inheritance such that every child receives a share of the property except in cases where a child's education for an urban career is financed by the family in lieu of a land share. Thus the exodus of one or more sons to diaspora centres reduced land fragmentation and, unlike the departure of landless villagers from other areas in Europe, was a counter to proletarianisation reducing the surplus agricultural population. In the context of *astifilia*, it fostered the association between urban employment and a rise in social status, since migration to urban diaspora centres nearly always resulted in the migrant's absorption into the middle class. Surprisingly, this occurred even when the labour recruited was not for middle-class jobs. Thus when 5,700 workers were recruited for the construction of the Suez Canal it was observed that most of these were either absorbed into the administrative or service sector or became independent artisans or small businessmen such as grocers.[35] Participation in Greek cultural institutions such as the church, the local Greek Association (*syllogos*) and schools, if they were parents, facilitated the emigrants' easy absorption into the Greek middle class, leaving manual labour to the illiterate locals.

The education system in the nineteenth century

An essential factor enabling those aspiring to move to urban middle-class employment was the early establishment of an extensive education network throughout Greece. Immediately following the War of Independence, there was no centrally organised educational system at all and it was President Kapodistrias' first priority to establish one. He declared: 'Greece's greatest hope is to be found in the education of her children.' Amongst the diaspora, education had been of prime importance for centuries. But as noted above it was only at the end of the eighteenth century that it became identified with Greece's liberation, at which point diaspora benefactors started donating very big sums towards the founding of schools. Many first-generation émigrés took pride in providing their village of origin with a school. Sometimes the financing of a school came from the local population itself and there are accounts of neighbouring villages competing with each other to raise local money to build schools. Remittances from émigrés in diaspora centres also helped to make this educational infrastructure possible. By 1830 there were 71 elementary schools with 6,000 pupils, equating to about eight per cent of primary-school-aged children. In 1834 the government declared that schooling was to be free to all and compulsory. Given the almost complete absence of government funds, this policy seemed more idealistic than practical. Astonishingly, however, by the 1860s the elementary school network had reached a level comparable to that of the industrialised European countries, with a quarter of primary-school-aged children from the agricultural population (85 per cent of the total population) catered for by this network. In 1864 there were almost as many boys in elementary education in Greece proportionately as in western Europe.[36] By 1889 there was one elementary school for every two villages.[37] The fact that most émigrés from rural Greece to Asia Minor were employed in middle-class work highlighted the value of education as a means to improving social status. To have established such an extensive elementary school network so soon after Independence and in such an impoverished country underlines the priority placed on education.

Still more striking was the secondary school network (consisting of middle school followed by gymnasium) founded in 1836. This was based on the French–Bavarian model and very quickly covered the whole of Greece; by 1855 there were over 5,000 middle school pupils out of a population of a million (cf. France in 1842 with 20,000 in a population of 20 million). In 1870 there was one gymnasium pupil for every 138 inhabitants (cf. France: 1/229; USA: 1/500), an unusually high percentage of children in secondary schools compared with western Europe, where secondary schools were mainly for the privileged few.[38] Finlay, the nineteenth-century British historian of Greece, notes that: 'The Greeks of every class have always set a higher value on a knowledge of letters than any other people. They have a national tendency to pedantism.'[39] In 1873, an American diplomat, Charles Tuckerman, observed that Greece was an over-educated country relative to its economic level, with an 'unnaturally' high number of secondary school pupils, as many poor as wealthy. He noted that Greece's education budget was very much higher than that of France, Italy, Germany or Austria.[40]

It was the scale of the diaspora funds that made this education network possible. For example, in 1880, the ten largest donations from abroad amounted to a larger sum than the entire state budget for education since Independence.[41] The democratic nature of secondary education, which was free, was striking both because of its very extensive and even distribution throughout the regions and because there was no two-tier academic/vocational system. Importantly, education in Greece did not begin in the towns and filter down to rural areas but began everywhere simultaneously. There was no correlation between the level of urbanisation in a region and the availability or level of schooling. *In fact, there was an inverse relation.* That is, there was a tendency for school attendance to be highest in areas of low urbanisation such as Lakonia and the Cyclades, areas where the small cultivator was predominant.

This contrasted with richer areas of commerce and export trade such as Corinth and Achaia where school attendance was lower. The rationale is clear when we look at the emigration rates and employment statistics for these regions. The small cultivator areas show a high rate of emigration and far higher representation in the civil service than richer areas where there would have been local employment opportunities that did not require educational qualifications.[42] On the basis of these developments one could see this trend as sowing the seeds of *astifilia* as an ideology of urban aspiration.

The War of Independence and the growth of Hellenism

In the end, the diaspora's wealth, their diminishing popularity outside Greece and their own growing nationalist sentiment provided the impetus for the re-establishment of Athens as the centre of Hellenism. Inspired partly by the French Revolution, Hellenism took root in diaspora communities and was an influential factor in the revolutionary movement within Greece. The absorption of Western liberal ideas by diaspora merchants in contact with the West and by Greeks educated at European universities fuelled a growing desire to liberate Greece politically and culturally from the Turks. Since all their assets were outside Greece the diaspora was not risking any material loss should the revolution fail. Adamantios Korais, a Greek intellectual from Smyrna who had settled in Paris, typified those who inspired by the French Revolution were now espousing Hellenism. His dream was to excise what he saw as the barbaric Ottoman heritage from Greece and to revive the culture and language of the ancient Greeks; in a word, to restore Greece's identity as the cradle of Western civilisation.

These westernising sentiments were not echoed within Greece either by the majority of the rich or at first by the poor, since neither of these groups stood to gain by the changes. The higher clergy, the landowners and the powerful tax-collecting class, all of whom occupied privileged positions under Ottoman rule, were naturally hostile both to westernisers and to the revolution. Similarly the small cultivators, though obviously keen to free themselves from the tyranny of the tax farmers, would have preferred to see a return to a strong Ottoman state as a safeguard of their traditional rights. By contrast, the artisans in textile manufacture and the workers in shipyards did constitute a significant revolutionary force. Their livelihoods had been lost both as a result of the English industrial revolution and due to the loss of provincial autonomy within Greece. Eventually even the cultivators, increasingly oppressed by the landowners and tax collectors, became inspired by the 'captains' (*kapetanaioi*). These were the mountain-based outlaws and rebels who represented opposition to established authority, in particular opposition to the tax-farmers, the *kotsabasides*. But notwithstanding these developments the uprisings of this active revolutionary force were mostly suppressed by the Ottoman authorities. The diaspora supporters of the revolution were forced to the conclusion that without foreign intervention the revolution could not succeed.

Initially the European powers, however, were most reluctant to interfere in the problems of the declining Ottoman Empire, for fear of upsetting the balance of power. Not until the British became afraid that Russia's influence in the Middle East would increase as a result of its relations with Greece was action taken. This rivalry between the powers was skilfully manipulated by the Greeks, resulting finally in Russia, Britain and France concluding the Treaty of London in 1827. The treaty guaranteed Greece's liberation though not her autonomy. Kapodistrias, a Corfiot in the Russian diplomatic service, was proclaimed president of Greece, a position he held until his assassination in 1831. His government's principal objective as related above was to eradicate the powers of the provincial oligarchies. In 1830, Russia's new policy of support for the preservation of the Ottoman Empire alarmed the English to the extent that they decided they had better go further than the 1827 treaty and give Greece complete independence. Complete independence that is from Turkey, but domination by all three of the Allies – a kind of protectorate status. In 1832 a monarch who was a neutral foreigner, Otho of Bavaria, was chosen as the best guarantor of internal unity and stability and a symbol for the Western models of government that it was hoped would be adopted.

From Ottoman control to virtual European protectorate

The degree of devastation, chaos and anarchy which characterised Greece in 1832 was seen as justification for the Bavarian regime's absolutist rule. A number of Bavarians and Frenchmen were employed in the higher levels of the state administration on the grounds that only Europeans could teach the Greeks civilised ways and, as outsiders, would stay clear of partisan strife. The strategy backfired, however, as the Bavarian government's absolutist policy was so draconian that after ten years it had united the Greek factions with the three foreign powers in opposition to it, resulting in its overthrow in 1843. The new all-party provisional government called for the election of a national assembly to draw up a constitution which would provide Greece with 'proper' parliamentary institutions. But the institutions imported wholesale from the West, instead of counteracting clientelist networks, meshed with the existing structures before an independent bureaucracy had had time to develop.[43] When universal male suffrage was introduced in 1864, Members of Parliament were able to draw on an even bigger supply of clients. Moreover, because demands were channelled into personal networks no strong interest groups or class-based associations formed, a significant contributor to subsequent developments. This atomising tendency was reinforced by the predominant land tenure system of small owner-cultivators (as opposed to latifundia).

The perception that government was the source of individual benefit, that bureaucrats were not impartial operators of neutral policies but rather handers-out of favours, increased the association between state employment and power. It must also have contributed to that mistrust in government institutions that has persisted into the twenty-first century. A mistrust which has fostered many of Greece's endemic problems from tax evasion (why pay when you believe government ministers will line their own pockets with your money?) to a cavalier attitude towards the legal system in general, which is recognised as un-transparent, convoluted and vulnerable to corrupt practice.

Emigration in preference to proletarianisation

The collapse of the market for Greek currants whose effects began to be felt in 1892 precipitated a slight increase in industrial dynamism by reducing the country's import potential and necessitating indigenous production as an alternative to currants.[44] Significantly, however, the larger-scale solution to the crisis was exodus because most of those hit by the disaster chose emigration over proletarianisation within Greece. Opportunities for emigration to Asia Minor and the Balkans were by this time greatly reduced as a result of growing nationalism in those regions and the transfer of many diaspora activities to Athens. Nor given the extent of the currant crisis could these traditional emigration centres have absorbed such large numbers. So the destination chosen was the USA. Strikingly, while the initial emigrants were those farmers immediately affected by the catastrophe, the movement rapidly spread to the whole population. In one generation, one-seventh of the entire Greek population, one-quarter of the workforce, left for the USA.[45] The annual average emigration from Greece to the USA from 1900 to 1910 numbered 25,000 people. In Yugoslavia it was 15,000, in Bulgaria 7,000,[46] even though those two countries unlike Greece suffered acutely from agricultural overpopulation. The fact that those two subsequently industrialised on a much larger scale than Greece strongly suggests that emigration, by removing a potential industrial workforce, was a major hindrance to industrialisation in Greece.

Greek emigration to the United States was quite different from the earlier migrations to diaspora centres, offering no prospect of a privileged position in the receiving society. Yet a study of what happened to these migrants reveals some common characteristics with earlier migrations. Firstly, more than any other migrants, Irish, Balkan or Italian, for example, Greeks showed an invariable preference for urban centres. By 1920 87.5 per cent of the first-generation migrants had settled in urban centres; by 1930, it was 91.3 per cent. Amongst the non-urban-dwelling migrants 0.1 per cent were in agricultural work. Secondly, after a first phase in which they worked in manual labour, the majority moved into small business and services; thousands worked in laundries, restaurants, tailoring and dressmaking establishments. They never joined the huge numbers of workers in industry. Thirdly, there was a very high literacy rate among migrants, much higher than that of all other nationals apart from the Irish, and higher than the average for Greece.[47]

Conclusion

At the start of this chapter, I asserted that the role of the diaspora was critical to Athens' atypical urban formation and the birth of *astifilia*. The diaspora's middle-class status in the host countries and its recruitment of employees from rural Greece were the basis for the early association between urban employment and absorption into the middle class. The growth of Hellenism led to the establishment by the diaspora of an extensive and democratic educational network within Greece. Growing nationalist feeling on the part of the host countries was a major reason for the subsequent transfer of many diaspora activities to Athens and the ensuing expansion of the public sector which provided the rural educated with urban middle-class jobs. Unfortunately for Greece's long-term economic development the diaspora continued to operate as middlemen rather than investing their very substantial capital in industrial ventures. This precluded the rise of an industrial proletariat and perpetuated Greece's dependence on foreign powers. Service sector employment, much of it in the public sector and most of it in Athens, together with emigration, continued to be the Greeks' preferred survival strategies.

CHAPTER 2

OBSTACLES AND DISINCENTIVES TO DEVELOPMENT IN MYSTRAS

Exodus

In the preceding chapter, I argued that Greece's poor economic development and low productivity owed a lot to the nineteenth-century diaspora's unwillingness to industrialise, to the role of clientelism in facilitating access to jobs in the public sector and to the consequent entrenchment of the ideology of *astifilia*. The resulting over-inflated size of the state apparatus and the absence of productive activity in Athens, where investment was largely concentrated in real estate, made the capital a centre of parasitism rather than an engine for growth.

In this chapter, I move to the twentieth century and to my fieldwork in the 1980s. Before getting to this point, however, we need to be aware of the level of social disintegration, political collapse and indebtedness experienced by Greeks following World War II and the Greek Civil War (1946–9). As a way of solving poverty and unemployment problems, postwar Greek governments encouraged emigration, and more than a million Greeks emigrated between 1950 and 1974; the census data for 1950–70 show that about a quarter of the entire active workforce left Greece over that period. Most went to western Europe, the USA, Canada and Australia. Economic and political reasons often motivated their move, both connected with the consequences of civil war and the 1967–74 period of military junta rule that followed. Official statistics show that in the period 1955–73 Germany absorbed 603,300 Greek migrants, Australia 170,700, the USA 124,000 and Canada 80,200, with the majority of these emigrants coming from rural areas. As in the currant-crisis years in the 1890s, when it was government policy to encourage villagers to migrate to Athens or abroad, and as in previous economic crises when there were too many jobless to be absorbed by the state sector, those without work chose emigration over manual work at home. Emigration plus a reduced birth rate from the 1950s onwards resulted in a perceptible drop in agricultural production.[1] By 1976 the loss of provincial population was on such a scale that a diminishing labour force and a serious and growing imbalance in population distribution – geographical and generational – had become a source of alarm to the authorities. At a social sciences conference on regional variation in Greece and Cyprus in 1976 the geographer Bernard Kayser, in a paper on the demographic decline of the Greek countryside, concluded: 'Three quarters of Greek national space is dying.'[2] Despite government plans for regional development drawn up in the 1970s, 487,000 villagers moved to Athens between 1970 and 1981. By 1981, 3,027,331 people – 31 per cent of the total population – were living in Athens, leaving the economic and social fabric of the provinces to deteriorate further.[3]

The ethnography and out-migration

Given this demographic background it is no surprise to find that most of the ethnographic studies made between 1950 and 1985 are concerned to some degree with the question of migration. Some studies focus more on the effects of depopulation on a community[4] while others focus more on the migrants.[5] A major motive for out-migration highlighted by the studies is the association between a move to Athens and a rise in social status. The American anthropologist Ernestine Friedl writes: 'At any level an occupation accrued greater prestige if it permitted life in Athens rather than in villages or provincial towns.' She observes that it was the better-off villagers who were most likely to leave.[6] Stanley Aschenbrenner makes the same point in his ethnography of Karpofora, an agricultural village in Messinia: 'By tradition, villagers were inclined to associate urban life, education, social status and wealth [...] Those remaining see themselves as behind, second rate and passed by.'[7] This in spite of the area's positive attributes:

> Due to its mild climate, fertile soil, and a considerable area with irrigation, it has a richer agricultural potential than many villages [...] Even with farming advantages and a favourable, accessible location, Karpofora has followed the general pattern of other far less blessed villages. It too has suffered depopulation through out-migration of adults and the current rejection of rural life by its youth [...] people have chosen to leave village life even though two apparently primary motives are lacking, namely, agricultural impoverishment and lack of modern amenities.[8]
>
> [...] The better life towards which parents and children direct resources and energies is cast entirely in terms of the city [...] They [the children] will leave regardless of improved conditions simply because *they have become conditioned to believe that to live in a village is to be old-fashioned and to be at the bottom of Greek society.*[9] [my italics]
>
> [...] During the past two decades [1970s and '80s], villagers have sought to improve their lives. Through success at this they have unintentionally fashioned a 'terminal' way of life that no longer meets the functional prerequisite of a

society. That is, it is failing to reproduce itself as a population and to perpetuate itself by enculturating the young as farmers. In this respect, the village follows a general pattern in rural Greece.[10]

The voluntary nature of urban migration is emphasised by anthropologists and sociologists alike.[11] They point out, as explained in the previous chapter, that Greek urban migration has little in common with the move to the city of a landless rural proletariat such as that found in southern Italy, Turkey or countries of the 'Third World'. A central explanatory factor in the ethnographic literature accounting for provincial exodus is this association between Athens and a rise in social status, an association that developed into an ideology I call *astifilia*.

1980s decentralisation

In 1981 the Greek Socialist Party (Pasok) led by Andreas Papandreou came to power, replacing Konstantinos Karamanlis' New Democracy party, which had reinstated democratic government following the overthrow of the Junta (1967–74). The Junta had fallen as a result of their abortive attempt to annex Cyprus to Greece, which in turn had led to the Turks' invasion and the island's division. In 1981, prior to the general election, Karamanlis had overseen the formal accession of Greece to the EEC as its tenth full member. This was more than a little controversial within the EEC since Greece was not considered economically strong, unsurprising bearing in mind that in 1976 the country was in debt to foreign lenders to the tune of US$2.2 billion. In fact the country had had a persistent balance-of-payments deficit since 1831. Nor, thanks to its recent history over Cyprus, was it regarded as particularly stable. But as with earlier and subsequent decisions relating to Greece's role in Europe, granting accession to the EEC in 1981 was a largely geopolitical decision. In this instance it was hoped that inclusion would avert a war with Turkey and strengthen Europe in this Cold War period.

When I started fieldwork in 1986 the demographic situation in Greece was changing. Pasok's accession to power coincided with the deep global recession of 1981–2, which was characterised by high unemployment in the West, making emigration from Greece more difficult. Greece's textile industry founded in 1923 by the Asia Minor refugees in a suburb of Athens, Nea Ionia, entered a period of crisis in the late 1970s and moved outside Europe. (It is significant that this industry was generated in the 1920s by newcomers.) At the same time becoming a full member of the EEC brought monetary transfers, in particular to the agricultural sector. Less positively, membership lifted protection from foreign food imports, which increased while Greek exports diminished, leaving Greece before long with an even more serious balance-of-payments deficit. This development led in 1984 to the need for an emergency loan from the EEC and the introduction of a tough Stabilisation Programme to deal with the crisis. Papandreou tried to impose a wage freeze – 'we can't keep on spending more than we produce' – but was met with strong resistance from the unions, and public debt continued to rise as the state sector expanded to combat unemployment. In 1985, an election year, when the current account deficit had reached a record level of $3.35 billion, the drachma was devalued and a draconian income policy put in place. The European Community held regular quarterly reviews, and strict limits were placed on pay increases in both the private and the public sectors. All of which will sound familiar to those who have followed developments in Greece since 2009. Indebtedness and dependency on foreign powers have been recurrent themes throughout Greece's modern history.

While the foregoing suggests a rather bleak scenario, a series of reforms introduced by Pasok had positive effects in the provinces, most notably the measures taken to tackle the problem of the over-centralised state. A core feature of Pasok's 1981 election campaign was decentralisation – *apokentrosis*. This was to be achieved through a regional development programme that aimed at 'the demographic and economic reconstruction' of the countryside and the promotion and development of medium-sized and small urban centres.[12] New laws were introduced assigning decision-making powers to local authorities which hitherto had only had consultative functions. New university departments were created in several provincial towns. The health service was reorganised so as to reduce the geographical imbalance of medical services. Efforts were made to improve recreational services in the provinces with the introduction of youth clubs, cultural centres and *kafeteria* for young people. A number of formerly isolated villages were linked by asphalt roads to regional centres. Simultaneously, increased government investment in agriculture together with EEC subsidies significantly strengthened the sector, leading to an improved infrastructure and rise in productivity. There had been a convergence of rural and urban living standards thanks to better road and transport communications, new electricity and piped water networks, as well as emigrant remittances to village families, enabling home improvements.

Throughout the 1980s the provincial population remained stable, the first decade not to register a decline. Two factors contributed to this stabilisation. First was the aforementioned world recession, which had reduced work opportunities abroad. Secondly, Athens was experiencing growing unemployment, higher rents and commodity costs as well as environmental problems such as severe air pollution. In light of these developments I hypothesised that the strengthening of the agricultural sector with substantial support from EEC subsidies might help to modify the influence of *astifilia*. Should the stringent economic reforms imposed by international creditors result in the required reduction of Greece's oversized bureaucracy, people would have to look elsewhere for work. Perhaps there would be a recognition in astifiliac villages that oversubscription to professional jobs had reached such proportions that alternative careers must be considered; in teaching, for example, a qualified teacher without political influence might wait up to ten years for a permanent post.

Up to this period many of the families living in areas of high emigration had been cushioned to some extent from current economic realities by foreign pensions. Returnees' American pensions were at least five times as much as a Greek farmer's pension of 12,000 drachmas a month and there were still many households receiving about £50 a month from relatives abroad. But as the old died and their pensions came to an end, as remittances diminished now that the cost of living for émigrés had risen, it was possible that young villagers might be spurred to look for income in areas such as commerce and agriculture. Attitudes towards the capital and the provinces might be altering in response to these changing circumstances and these would be reflected in new economic strategies, demographic patterns and social activities.

Mystras

I chose the area of Sparta in Lakonia, the southernmost province of the Peloponnese, to do fieldwork. It was at once a fertile centre of agriculture on the small cultivator pattern and an area with a long history of emigration. If attitudes towards town and country were changing, there would be scope in this area for agricultural expansion. The village where I started my fieldwork, Mystras (population in the 1980s *c.*700), lies five kilometres west of Sparta, the provincial capital, in the foothills of the Taygetos mountains at a height of 320 metres. The village is in the centre of an orange- and olive-growing area and well watered. Just above the main village is the outstandingly beautiful semi-ruined Byzantine city of Mystras. So there was no shortage of local resources to exploit should the previous five years since Pasok's introduction of *apokentrosis* and less auspicious conditions in Athens have led to changed attitudes. After several months' fieldwork I had found little evidence for new economic initiatives; the village's development echoed in many respects that of the villages studied in the earlier ethnography on Greece. Emigration abroad had been very high, and continued albeit on a much smaller scale; aspiration for public sector jobs in the fire service, banking, police, education or in law and medicine was very pronounced; interpersonal relations were difficult.

Although there was a preponderance of elderly and middle-aged villagers, Mystras' viability had never been in question since people from a number of higher villages, some now abandoned, had moved down in the 1960s and 1970s. In addition, a third of the population in the 1980s were returnees from abroad. Towards the end of the 1980s, there was a slight shift in favour of Sparta as a locus for work in preference to Athens, but urban white-collar jobs in the public sector, whether in Athens or Sparta, remained most villagers' goal, if not for themselves then for their children. Local resources, agricultural and commercial, were underexploited, while social institutions were conservative with a marked age–gender hierarchy. Of Mystras' population, 65–70 per cent had left the village in the 1950s and 1960s. The majority went to Canada and the USA, while a smaller number went to Australia. Those who emigrated had little land; families were often large, and partible inheritance had led to fragmentation of landholdings. Moreover, the larger portion of arable land was concentrated in the hands of a few wealthy families. This unequal distribution of land had enabled the large landowners to employ poorer villagers as sharecroppers. A similar employment pattern wherever terrain was suitable for intensive cultivation could be observed all over the province. It is probably no coincidence that in such areas the civil war was experienced more bitterly and more intensely than elsewhere. Shortage of land, and unequal distribution of favours by large landowners, put a strain on social relations. The situation must have been much like that described by one of Anna Collard's informants for Evritania, central Greece: 'People used the civil war to fight out personal animosities and hostilities, that was the worst. People who didn't like each other before or had some long standing complaint or quarrel with one another, used this as a basis for killing and fighting each other.'[13] The generation which in the 1980s was in its thirties was said to be the first to feel detached from the bitternesses engendered by the civil war. When American and Canadian immigration policy provided an opportunity for exodus in the 1950s and 1960s it is not surprising that the villages which had experienced the worst traumas of the Civil War, intensified by pre-existing conditions of scarcity and oppression, should opt for emigration on a large scale. Those villagers who remained continued to work for the large landowners. But with a depleted workforce the landowners' position weakened until, as villagers in the 1980s recalled, 'It was their turn to come knocking on *our* doors.' Gradually the landowning families left for Athens, partly so that their children could study at the university, partly because labour became too expensive for farming to be profitable. In some cases estate owners rented out their land, in others they sold all or part of it.

The higher villages

Emigration to the USA and Canada from the higher villages above Mystras, while not on the same scale, was as high as 50 per cent in the 1950s and 1960s. It was motivated by different considerations more to do with geography. Unlike Mystras, which from the early nineteenth century had a good road to Sparta, these villages were all at the end of steep mule tracks, and accessibility was a problem. Relations of production had differed from those in Mystras chiefly because the steepness of the terrain was unsuitable for extensive agriculture. Villagers had combined small-scale herding and olive

39

cultivation with woodcutting, ladder making and charcoal burning. Subsistence agriculture and the sale of livestock products to lower villages without flocks, the sale of wood, charcoal and ladders, had enabled them to live more independently than the Mystriots. Some men from these villages had gone as target migrants to New York at the beginning of the twentieth century. Those who came back rich were known as *Brooklides* (having made good in Brooklyn). A number were said to have buried part of their money when they returned, rather than entrusting it to banks, and some of their descendants in the 1980s had not given up hope of finding it.

In contrast to the Mystriot emigrants, most of whom settled abroad permanently, higher-village populations followed several different strategies. A number accumulated sufficient capital abroad to invest in real estate and by the 1980s owned property in Athens. Others emigrated permanently while most of those who had remained in the higher villages eventually moved down the mountain to settle in Mystras. By the end of the 1960s some villages had emptied out. Incomers from the more accessible higher villages retained their land above and continued to cultivate their olive trees and vines. On moving to Mystras they began to acquire small parcels of land from the departing big landowners. By contrast, very few Mystriots returning from abroad invested in agricultural land or in any local commercial venture, preferring to invest in real estate in Athens or Sparta. Mystriots who had settled abroad usually held on to their houses in the village, leaving what land they had in the hands of relatives and their houses empty. I was struck in the 1970s and 1980s by the large number of closed houses there were in these villages.

Economic opportunities undermined by emigration

In 1960 an important change in production occurred when a new source of water was found, making orange cultivation possible. Until this period the chief crops had been olives, wheat, figs, grapes and silkworm cocoons. Wheat had ceased to be planted as relatively cheap imports of cereals increased and ready-made bread could now be bought. The cocoon industry, which depended on mulberry tree cultivation, had been supplanted by the artificial silk industry. The trade agreement made in the 1930s between Metaxas' government and Germany for the export of figs to Germany ended in the 1950s and the market for figs collapsed. Vines are labour-intensive several times a year; olive trees require five or six times the amount of land required for orange trees to produce the same annual income and, unlike orange trees which produce uniformly each year, olive trees produce abundantly alternate years only. Furthermore, oranges require far less labour than olives: no regular pruning and a harvest time of two days as opposed to three months. Thus to own a piece of land suitable for an orange grove became every family's ambition. Opportunities for suitable land were limited since the land had to be within reach of water for summer irrigation, as well as level and in a frost-free situation, but many villagers acquired at least a small grove.

Not many families in the 1960s could earn enough from olive and orange cultivation alone unless they combined it with non-agricultural employment or seasonal work at the lime kilns or olive presses. The chief source of non-agricultural employment in the 1960s was the construction industry, which enjoyed a boom following the earlier postwar depression. Men found jobs in sand quarries and cement manufacture as well as in building. But the difficulty in finding permanent employment in an area where the secondary sector was so underdeveloped had two consequences. Villagers continued to emigrate throughout the 1960s, and those who remained either educated their children for urban jobs if they showed any scholastic aptitude or encouraged them to emigrate. The unstable nature of the secondary sector as a supplementary source of work, plus the almost complete absence of state welfare, led to intensified efforts by villagers to enter public sector jobs. These represented both security, understandably a central preoccupation, and social status. The consequences of these strategies were very significant for Mystras' later development. They resulted in the prolonged education of the majority of young people, many of whom left the village in the 1970s, thus skewing the age distribution. Those young men who remained were not interested in agriculture, while some young women instead of marrying into similar orange-growing villages – the pattern in the 1960s and 1970s – now aspired to marry to Athens or Sparta, increasing the loss of young from these villages.

In light of Pasok's policies vis-à-vis the provinces and new incentives for agricultural engagement, one might have expected a shift in attitude in favour of agriculture and village life such as recorded in other countries – by the ethnographers Weinberg and Cole and Wolf for alpine regions;[14] or, for Hungary (Reining, Andorka and Harcsa);[15] or, for Spain (Douglass)[16] – where young people saw the benefits of occupational diversification. In these examples young men combined small-scale agriculture both for subsistence and market with salaried work elsewhere. In Weinberg's village of Bruson, agriculture and pastoralism were supplemented by the introduction of new market crops and opportunities for wage labour in the valley below. There were entrepreneurial experiments such as an attempt to build up a ski resort. Interestingly, although in Bruson, as in Greek villages like Mystras, education was the accepted way to social mobility, Brusonins had come to see education as leading to a forfeiture of independence because it involved leaving the village, renting accommodation expensively and spending more on consumption.[17] In Greece in the 1980s I speculated that since oversubscription to professional and civil service jobs was acute there might be a comparable shift away from the focus on education and state employment.

Opportunities, thanks to favourable ecological, geographical and historical factors, were conducive to development. The village's position in the Taygetos foothills in the shadow of the steep east-facing forested mountains meant that its terrain was well watered. The impregnability of one of these foothills, a fortress-like rocky hill, had led to its becoming the Byzantine capital of the Peloponnese. Thus in the 1980s Mystras had three valuable assets: fertile terrain; a spectacular Byzantine site to draw tourists; and easy access to Sparta, the capital and administrative centre of the province with its facilities for education, healthcare and commercial activity such as marketing produce. There was no sign, however, of a Brusonin-type change in strategy in Mystras or in other villages which had experienced high emigration in the province. Parents continued to make education for professional or office jobs their children's first priority. Children who failed university entrance the first time were encouraged to study at home for another year and try again. Of Mystras' 50 young men aged between 18 and 35, two were engaged in some way in agriculture, two were shepherds. No others under 60 did agricultural work. One of the young men was described as too stupid to do anything else. The other, whose family was from a higher village, was exceptional because he hired himself out with his tractor, combining this work with helping his parents in the family restaurant – exactly the kind of mixed economic strategy one might have expected.

Obstacles and disincentives to economic development

To make sense of Mistriots' resistance to opportunities at home I set out to identify the disincentives beyond the ideological pull of the capital's route to social prestige and emigration, the fallback solutions to distaste for village life. The link with Canada and the USA may have put a dampener on local initiative as these countries were not only a source of remittances and pensions, but could still be resorted to for employment, healthcare, marriage partners and higher education if necessary. Moreover, the USA and Canada were the chief source of savings that enabled returnees to invest in Greek urban property – an important source of rentier income for about a third of the village's population in the 1980s. A major disincentive lay in the bias favouring office work and the opportunities for such work in Sparta despite oversubscription and despite its not being Athens. In 1990 when OTE, the state telephone company, held examinations, 500 candidates competed for three posts. The means by which such jobs were obtained, political clientelism, connections – *meson* – actually perpetuated parents' ambitions for their children as experience showed that *meson* were a more effective instrument for obtaining employment than meritocratic means.

Turning to the locally available sources of income, I looked at each in turn to see what might be the pros and cons. Orange cultivation had been dubbed *astiki douleia* – town work – because once established it required less labour than other crops. Regular watering was essential of course; but wealthy town dwellers were installing mechanical watering systems operated from their homes, while the two-day harvest was done by hired workers, usually migrant labour from poor areas of northern Greece like Trikala. By the 1980s, however, irrigation was becoming an issue. Except in areas where water was exceptionally abundant it was expensive and subject to seasonal scarcity. In all areas near Sparta where there was well-watered, frost-free level ground, water shortages, sometimes permanent, had begun to arise as orange grove planting had expanded. In Mystras, irrigation for most was from community water and operated on a rota system. The water came from a mountain spring, which reached the orange grove through a network of *avlakia*, water channels. The orange grove cultivator had to dig channels in his grove so that the water reached every tree. The flow of the water was rather slow, and watering a four-stremmata orange grove took at least six hours. Although watering only had to be done in the summer months, it had to be done on average every ten days and rotas meant having to use night hours as well. The operation was hard physical work and especially unpleasant on night shifts. Fighting for day shifts, allegations of exceeding the allotted hours or stealing the water from an earlier point in the channel were some of the causes leading to frustration with the community system. The alternative to using community water was to own a well accessible to the grove. Well owners could water when they chose and had the advantage of greater water pressure, which reduced watering time by two-thirds. They could install an automatic watering system using a system of pipes linked to each individual tree. For owners of large orange groves, eight stremmata or more, this was in the long run the cheaper and most labour-saving solution. The problem was that installing a well required capital of at least four million drachmas (c.£13,000).

Two issues were involved here. One concerned the logistics of making a well, the other the ownership of the grove. Many orange grove buyers in the 1960s were emigrants who saw the groves as a good investment for their return. They left the cultivation of the groves in the care of relatives or friends. About a third of the villagers cultivated oranges in groves belonging to relations who had settled permanently abroad. The cultivator as opposed to the owner was entitled to the profits but was also responsible for the outgoings. Since there was never any guarantee that the absentee owner would not decide to sell, cultivators were reluctant to make any but the most essential investments such as applying fertiliser and watering. They were certainly not going to risk investing capital in the installation of a well or a mechanical watering system. When freak conditions in March 1987 killed large numbers of orange trees, caretaker cultivators did not replace the dead trees, a good example of how large-scale emigration can affect a community's long-term productivity.

The second issue, the logistics of well installation, was problematic even for grove owners partly because of the capital expenditure involved. A few villagers reduced this by sharing the costs with a close neighbour, but not many villagers had neighbours with whom they wished to share. Then there was always a risk that several searches would have to be made before a water source was located, adding to the expense. The best solution was to apply for EEC improvement scheme funds, which covered 50 per cent of the costs. This required the applicant to submit plans for the watering system, which presupposed a good head for figures and most likely political connections as well. Bureaucracy at the overmanned offices of the Agricultural Advisory Service in Sparta does not operate straightforwardly. Obstructionist tactics and demands for bribes are par for the course, and the implementation of the law is complicated by the unclearness of many laws. Bureaucratic hurdles of the kind propagated by the Agricultural Advisory Service have long been an impediment to initiative, productivity and responsiveness to change all over the province. The American political scientist Keith Legg wrote of Greece in 1969:

> The contemporary legal system, with a civil law based on conflicting Byzantine sources, a nineteenth century commercial code ill adapted to its new environment, plus adaptations of more recent foreign codes masquerading as legal reforms, is characterised by complexity and intense conflict. The codes may have originally been prescriptive in character; but decades of training in jurisprudence have produced a bureaucracy that judges all activity by its conformity to regulations, even contradictory ones. There is a constant need for new legislative enactments, ministerial decrees, and administrative rulings to fill in gaps or adjust conflicts in the existing laws. Thorough legislative reform in any area is discouraged; instead minor adjustment or alteration is the rule. These conditions encourage particularistic bureaucratic treatment and constant political interference in the administrative world.[18]

The situation more than half-a-century later has not improved and is graphically (and tragicomically) portrayed by Panayotis

Karkatsoulis of the Athens School of Public Administration in his lectures on *polinomia* and the monster state. Illustrating the dysfunctional nature of the monster he gives this example: 'If I host a picnic in the forest and want to be sure I am complying with current fire safety regulations, I have to contact eleven different government agencies or officials.' These include the Defence Ministry, the Air Force, the Culture Ministry and the local forest ranger. Expanding on the theme, he notes that the central administration comprises a grand total of about 23,000 different responsibilities: rules, restrictions, prohibitions. Furthermore, the responsibilities in the governmental structures are constantly changing, on average 1,140 times a year.[19]

In view of these conditions, one can see why villagers hesitated to get involved with bureaucracy and why the most economical way to install the most efficient type of watering system was daunting to many. The villagers best equipped educationally to cope with the bureaucrats were the young, the very section of the population that had no agricultural experience and no commitment to agriculture. For these reasons orange cultivation in Mystras was neither as modernised nor as productive as it might have been.

Olive cultivation

Every Mistriot owned some olive trees, enough in most cases to meet domestic consumption needs. The average landholding was about 24 stremmata (2.4 hectares) normally in four or five parcels. Some of these properties were inherited and situated in higher villages as well as in Mystras. Others had been acquired within the village in the 1960s. A few wives owned dowry groves in their villages of origin (marriage had been exclusively exogamous for the past 40 years) but many of these groves were sold, deemed too distant to be practicable economically. For the previous ten years (up to the mid-1980s) dowries had been in cash rather than land, an indication of changed priorities. Three or four families rented land from absentee landowners but they were not going to risk investing in land that might be sold or taken back at any time; so as long as absentees did not sell, redistribution and consolidation of land did not take place. Those few villagers who owned larger properties were obliged to take on extra labour as they were elderly and their children worked in Athens. There was very little locally available labour; none of the unemployed youth, male or female, waiting to re-sit university entrance exams or to enter the army engaged in wage labour of any kind, whether this was harvesting oranges or olives or assisting on local building jobs.

The labour question was the main problem for olive cultivators. In predominantly agricultural communities in the 1980s where the unit of production was the owner-family and harvesting could be done by family members alone, it was not necessary to calculate labour costs and picking could be done over an extended period at the family's convenience. For Mystriots engaged in non-agricultural labour, picking had either to be done outside work hours or by retired family members. Unlike the harvested oranges, which were collected, weighed and paid for by the juice factory, olives had to be taken to a press where the press owner levied 11 per cent of the oil before selling it for the cultivator. This process could take up to a year as the press owner waited for the best price.

A further disincentive to olive cultivation in Mystras was its old-fashioned nature. Because many properties were small and land parcels scattered it was not worth the owners' while to invest in mechanisation or in systemisation of planting and cultivation techniques. There had been no new planting over the past decade and as ploughing and spreading of fertiliser had to be done by hired labour because few locals owned tractors, the expense discouraged villagers from ploughing as often as required. Pruning the trees (calculated by the Agricultural Bank as requiring eight hours' labour per stremma per year) was often neglected, as few other than elderly locals knew how to do it. As a result, productivity was much lower than it need have been.

Marketing was also inefficient because oil was individually sold and quantities were small. One solution would have been to establish a village olive cooperative. Several attempts were made and failed. One problem arose from the law, which stipulated that the administrative officers of a cooperative must have agriculture as their first occupation. The only valid candidates were elderly villagers, most of whom were functionally illiterate. Moreover, the leading opponent of the projected cooperative was the former mayor and owner of the non-cooperative olive press. Nevertheless, a successful application was eventually made to the government, which agreed to donate seven million drachmas and to loan the remainder of 20 million. However, the former mayor was able to invoke a law that he claimed made the establishment of a cooperative oil press illegal. This was on the basis that if the village had an oil press that had been modernised before the cooperative application was registered the application was invalidated. The actual dates were in dispute but the ultimate decision was in the hands of the side that could invoke more powerful political influence. No cooperative oil press was set up.

Under-exploitation of a non-agricultural resource: Old Mystras

The site of the Byzantine capital of the Peloponnese was an important potential source of income to the village. It lies one kilometre to the north of the present village in a spectacular position further up the mountainside. While most of the secular buildings were left in ruins by the Turks in 1820, many of the churches survived. This ghost town in a lush setting full of flowers (in spring) and cypress trees is outstandingly beautiful. For several reasons it was late in becoming a serious tourist attraction.

Initially the prejudice in favour of ancient Greek ruins of the classical and Mycenaean period caused its neglect. The Bavarian kings who ruled Greece in the nineteenth century were foremost promoters of this neglect, to the extent that King Otho insisted on the removal of the provincial capital from Mystras to the site of ancient Sparta. Sparta represented a part of Greece's illustrious past, its former glory as the cradle of civilisation. Despite strong local opposition by the rich Mystriot families, a neo-classical city was built on the indistinct foundations of ancient Sparta, and Old Mystras was left to crumble further into ruins. A popular dystich lamented Mystras' fate:

Parori me ta kria nera, ki Ayanni mou me t'anthi,
Kai si kakomire Mystras, se halase i Sparti.

Parori with her cold waters, Ayanni with her flowers,
But you, unfortunate Mystras, have been ruined by Sparta.

Not until more than a century later were steps taken to reinstate Byzantine monuments. In 1953, the Greek Archaeological Authorities decided to evacuate Old Mystras, then inhabited by 35 families (160 people), in order to begin restoration work. Some of these families were refugees from other areas including, some claimed, escaped criminals from Kalamata prison. They formed the underclass of village society by virtue of their extreme poverty, a significant contributor probably to the negative image the site retained in village consciousness.

In the 1960s a government-owned chain, the Xenia, opened a restaurant on the road not far from the site. At about the same time, a returnee from America bought the café by the lower entrance to the site, ideally placed to cater to tourists. To preclude further competition, he made use of a powerful local Member of Parliament to get a law passed forbidding any further building in this area; a law ostensibly invoked to preserve the environment close to an ancient monument. It is claimed that a few years later he did not vote for this MP, who consequently engineered the cafe's closure for several years. A year or two after the cafe reopened, a local Mystriot couple in their fifties surprised the village by setting up a drinks stall outside the main upper gate to the site. Immediately, the owner of the now-reopened cafe started a lawsuit against them claiming that their stall was infringing the preservation-of-the-environment order and/or was a health risk. After a six-month legal battle, during which time the stall was not allowed to operate, the stall owners won their case. These kinds of political machinations were continuous, an illustration of the kinds of obstacles new initiatives were up against.

Before Pasok came to power, the Byzantine site had not been a major source of employment. Half-a-dozen guards and two or three labourer-restorers worked there with all three entrance gates open. In 1981, with a change of government there was a change of policy. The lowest gate, the Marmara Gate, the first one to be reached from the village and the most convenient entrance for walkers, was closed, due it was claimed to shortage of personnel. Simultaneously, paradoxically, a much larger number of site staff were taken on, all Pasok voters, from this area well known for its right-wing, often Monarchist, population. Subsequently political clientelism enabled still further increases in personnel which by the end of the 1980s had reached a total of 60 (not all Mystriots), thereby increasing the Socialist vote in a bastion of New Democracy.

The Archaeological Authority

The local office of the Byzantine Archaeological Authority is in Sparta. Mystriots used to admiringly observe that the head of the authority had such powerful connections that they could retain the job even through changes of government. The influence exercised by this authority was a major issue for anyone wishing to make changes locally, be that to a private individual's house, a community project to put up a bus shelter, or a commercial enterprise. It is the Archaeological Authority's job to preserve a suitable environment in the region of the site. However, the same kind of political manoeuvring and arbitrary interpretations of the law as seen in the context of the Agricultural Advisory Board operated here. Thus one man could alter his house or open a restaurant while another with similar plans could not. The consequences of this particularistic policy and unpredictable interpretation of the law were twofold. They were the source of bitter antagonisms between villagers and they put a severe brake on local initiatives of a commercial nature.

Within the new village there was a hotel for tourists, constructed during the building boom of the 1960s. It was owned and run by a widow and her grown-up children, who struggled to make it profitable. This was partly because business was seasonal, partly because few visitors to the site chose to remain in the village. Tourists only stay by the sea, said Mystriots. There was an element of self-fulfilling prophecy here since the cafes and restaurants, along with the grocers, made little effort to attract tourists or to offer a high level of service. This attitude probably stemmed from the unambitious nature of small businesses within the village. One shop which also served as post office was run by a returnee in his sixties who drew an American pension. His only child was a bank clerk in Sparta (a state job with tenure) and married. The shop was run more as a pastime and social centre for a few elderly men than for profit and sold little beyond soap powder and the odd tin. The other shop, while stocking more, was equally circumscribed in its level of service.

The clientele of the two Mystras cafes largely reflected Civil War divisions. This source of disunity from the 1940s, when Civil War enmities here had been manifested in a particularly high level of bloodshed, still survived. Young men preferred to socialise in Sparta, where they could avoid politics and find mixed company. Women and girls in Mystras did not use the public space of the village for socialising and avoided the square if possible, sending children to the shops when necessary and making detours if they had to cross the village. A woman waiting for a bus to Sparta would wait in a side street off the central square until the bus came. The low visibility of women was striking.

In the late 1980s there were new initiatives in Mystras. A Greek entrepreneur with international experience in the hotel business and a chain of hotels in Greece bought the ruins of the once-imposing Sassendas mansion, whose heirs had emigrated to America. The mansion was restored and was expected to be in operation as a 50-room hotel by 1992. Such an initiative was easier for an outsider to launch both because of his substantial capital and experience in the business and because a non-Mystriot was less vulnerable to partisan local opposition. However, the project did not come to fruition and despite several changes of ownership was still not functioning more than a quarter-of-a-century later.[20] Restaurants, like the cafes and shops, catered to tourists in the tourist seasons, but had limited aims and showed very little entrepreneurial initiative: 'We just want to make enough money to pay for our daughter's dowry flat and then we'll probably stop.' Or: 'It's just something for my husband to do since he retired from working at the site.'

One new initiative despite opposition from many sides did eventually succeed. A returnee from New York resettled in Mystras in 1980, practising in Sparta as a dental technician. In 1986 he conceived the idea of opening a camping site with pool just below the village, where he owned an olive grove. Initially, the project would be largely financed by a loan from the Greek Tourist Board. The first attack on the project came from the Archaeological Authorities. With the help of political connections this problem was relatively easily overcome since the applicant had run as Socialist candidate for mayor in the 1983 local elections. However, the olive press owner, who was mayor at the time and a member of the opposition New Democracy party, filed a suit against the applicant claiming that it was illegal to build on land so close to the site of the village's annual fair. With the advantage of a Socialist government in power the returnee dentist overcame this problem albeit after a protracted battle. He then had to engage with a large number of other authorities. To negotiate successfully with each set of bureaucrats it was felt necessary to have a personal connection in each office; for example, a relative who as secretary could see that the file was placed near the top of a pile. In 1988 permission was finally granted and the project was completed. This triggered a campaign by villagers who wished to see the enterprise fail. The signs advertising the camp were removed; the official bus stop was shifted so that tourists travelling by bus from Sparta never learnt that there was a campsite. Yet village restaurants, cafes and shops stood to gain from campsite visitors. The reaction recalled the Limited Good thesis of the anthropologist George Foster[21] – the perception that someone else's success could only be at another's expense, a zero-sum game; a subject I return to in the next section.

Sparta

Mystras as noted had three main assets: its fertile terrain; the archaeological site; and closeness to Sparta – a source of education, medical treatment and state sector employment (Sparta's official population in the late 1980s was 13,000.) The hospital, the fire service, the forestry commission and the archaeological museum in Sparta were grossly overmanned as MPs created positions in exchange for votes. The supposedly stringent economic reforms imposed by international creditors were being ignored with impunity. The number of private cramming establishments, many owned by qualified teachers who had failed as yet to secure positions in schools, ran into hundreds thanks to oversubscription to the profession. Apart from a seasonally operating orange juice factory employing a dozen workers in winter only, and one or two small-scale marble and cement quarries, there was no industry. The fruit canning factory was derelict since business had been moved several years earlier to Patras. There were numerous doctors, lawyers and notary offices, two private clinics, several private blood-testing laboratories, two private X-ray centres, 20 chemists and a large number of small shops, cafes and bars, all family-run. Apart from the museum and a public library closed for three years because of a property dispute, Sparta had little to offer in the way of entertainment or intellectual stimulus. There was little to act as a catalyst for change and much to discourage change. Some years before, a New Democracy mayor had been instrumental in turning down a proposal that the Pedagogic Academy should be opened in Sparta. He had argued that an influx of students from other provinces might corrupt Lakonian youth. The academy was subsequently established in Tripolis, 30 miles to the north.

Sparta was traditionally Monarchist, probably a legacy from King Otho's creation of the town. The area had a reputation in Athens for being hyper-conservative, reactionary and narrow-minded. As related in the first chapter, large numbers of Lakonians had been moving to Athens to work in civil service jobs since the nineteenth century. Now in the 1970s and 1980s the gradual backflow of émigrés from Canada and the USA (perhaps not sufficiently well off to build in Athens) had given rise to a construction boom as returnees used their savings to build dowry flats for their daughters or apartment blocks as sources of rent. Building licences issued by the Town Planning Office in Sparta indicated that at least 50 per cent of apartment blocks were built by returnees or 'commuter' American/Canadian Greeks. These activities, however, injected no long-term dynamism into the economy or life of the town. In fact, the returnees who made up a third or more of the population in the 1980s were the most conservative element. During their period abroad in the USA or Canada they had lived in ghettos often with Greeks from the same province or even the same village. The local Greek Orthodox Church was their social centre and promoter of Greek cultural activities such as traditional dancing and cuisine. For these émigrés Greek culture had been preserved in crystallised form; they were hardly aware of the political and socio-economic changes occurring in their absence within Greece. Once back in Sparta, thanks to their foreign savings returnees enjoyed high status largely derived from visible manifestations of their wealth such as smart dress, cars and luxuriously appointed apartments. The presence of these returnees, few of whom if any invested in long-term commercial enterprises, contributed both to Sparta's conservatism and to its prestigious image in the view of urban-oriented villagers, an image reflected in villagers' ambition to work in Sparta and if possible to live there. It was reflected in the number of dowry flats built by village parents wishing their daughters to move to a 'better life' and in the preference for celebrating weddings and baptisms in Sparta. Sparta churches were urban and hence had more social cachet than village churches. As in the dystich, Sparta had superseded many of the village's functions in such a way as to rob Mystras of much of its dynamism.

CHAPTER 3

SOCIAL RELATIONS
IN MYSTRAS

Emigration and stagnation

Large-scale out-migration influences the social dynamic in a community as those individuals more likely to act as agents for change are usually the ones to leave. This leads to loss of dynamism and, perhaps less obviously negative, to a reduction in intergenerational conflict. If conflict is instrumental in bringing about change, exodus of a sizable proportion of the young risks a reinforcement of the pre-existing order.[1] The anthropologist John Davis discusses this theme and the role of the relations between generations in Lison-Tolosana's *Belmonte de los Caballeros*:

> The generations were in important respects in opposition to each other, perhaps partly because of their experiences as emergers under the control of their predecessors. And their reactiveness influenced their actions: they created new conditions, new environments to which in due course their successors would react in their turn [...] each new generation takes its inheritance from its predecessor, reacts against it and, in response to 'the historical situation', creates

a new environment that again is the object of reaction. The dynamo of history, in Belmonte in the period 1900–61, was the reactive reinterpretation of events; and the social relations that produce the history (and further events) were primarily those of opposition or even hostility between generations.[2]

Precisely this reaction against 'the controlling generation'[3] was absent in Mystras, where out-migration had left community elders to perpetuate the traditional order. *Astifilia* with its emphasis on higher education and urban jobs was not the only value which seemed to have been reinforced as a result of emigration. Paradoxically, given the local association between participation in urban life and modernity, patriarchal values relating to age and gender hierarchy predominant in the 1950s and 1960s had persisted into the 1980s. One contributory factor was the gradual disengagement from agriculture which reduced women's participation, increasing their economic dependence and social isolation. As long as subsistence agriculture continued to be important, wives had a central and vital function in the household and a role which brought them into contact with their adopted (marriage was exogamous) community. In the 1980s, women in their fifties and sixties recalled earlier communal activities and exchange of work. For instance, wheat which was planted by individual families until the beginning of the 1970s was harvested by groups of women working on each other's fields in turn. Staples such as *hilopites*, the local pasta made from wheat flour, milk and eggs, were produced at each family's house in turn by a group of women. The immediate neighbourhood (*yitonia*) was an important centre of companionship, with women gathering in their free time to talk while their children played nearby. As late as 1978 these neighbourhood gatherings (*rouga*) still took place, as I had witnessed myself. However, villagers told me in the mid-1980s that contact between neighbours had now greatly diminished.

They attributed this decrease in neighbourhood socialising to the advent of television, increased car ownership and falling numbers of children. These factors certainly played a role, but the most significant cause was probably the change in women's function once agriculture had ceased to be their main occupation. Wheat cultivation, for example, ceased in the 1970s when it became cheaper to buy ready-made bread; livestock breeding diminished in all but the poorest families as fodder production was seen as too troublesome without machinery and too small-scale to warrant mechanisation. Increased prices for olive oil and oranges in the 1970s, plus generous remittances at this period from emigrant kin, improved most families' finances, blunting motivation for subsistence agriculture. Additional factors militated against the earlier, more intensive contact between villagers: the exodus of Mystriots to transatlantic destinations or Athens and, perhaps less foreseeably, the influx of returnees. In the latter case this was because feelings of relative deprivation tended to arise where differences in income, manifested in returnees' houses, their interior decoration and luxury items, became apparent. A returnee who had invested in real estate in Athens or had a foreign pension could enjoy a higher standard of living than a villager who had stayed in the village.

Despite the reduction in women's work as a result of agricultural disengagement and the substantial improvement in village standards of living, mothers were determined that their daughters should achieve something better than village life, still closely associated with dirt, hard work and backwardness. To this end, many parents from the 1970s onwards aimed to save enough to invest in an urban dowry flat so that their daughters could move to a better life, *'paei ya kalitera'*, when they married. This decision led to the establishment of new marriage patterns, which became especially marked in the 1980s. The majority of marriages were still arranged through intermediaries – *sinoikesion/proxenio* – who might be relations or acquaintances. But now the exchange of brides between these villages in the Taygetos foothills brought new brides less frequently to the village, instead removing the grooms to Sparta where the new bride's dowry came in the form of a flat.

While agricultural disengagement, diversification of occupation, differences in income, experience and education meant greater isolation for women, men's community life was much less affected. One factor contributing to women's greater isolation was exogamy since, unlike the men, most of whom had grown up together, the married-in women had fewer opportunities now for getting to know each other. The sexual division of leisure that enabled men to meet casually in the public space of the village square kept women at home so that socialisation could only take place by crossing the threshold of each other's houses. Once status distinctions entered into community relations, threshold crossing became problematic.

The invisibility of women generally in these villages was remarkable. Only the 'not quite respectable' women were visible. These were the wives of the café owners who helped day and night in these exclusively male meeting places. They were at the bottom of the social and moral scale, lower than shepherds' wives, whose work with animals was socially demeaning but morally acceptable. By contrast, the shopkeepers' wives, who were considered to be highly respectable, were never seen in the streets or in the family shop. Women avoided passing through the agora, the central square, both when crossing the village and, as related above, when waiting for the bus to Sparta. Young women in Mystras were embarrassed to walk through the agora because there were invariably a dozen or so men sitting at cafe tables staring at anyone who passed through. Only where religious rites were involved, such as carrying the memorial food (*koliva/stari*) from a mourner's house to the graveyard, would groups of women use the central road. It was acceptable for a woman to use this route to get to church on Sunday mornings, but if possible she would make a detour or find a neighbour to go with. Once she reached the church a woman on her own might linger outside in the hope that someone else would turn up so they could go in together. This would at least divide the attention of those women inside who closely scrutinised each new arrival's clothes. The standards were set by a group of older women who lived in an area of the village known locally as Kolonaki after the elegant district in Athens. Not being smart enough or somehow getting it wrong and provoking ridicule was a source of anxiety. The best defence was minute conformity to locally dictated fashion.

The dictatorship of conformity meant that an in-marrying bride in 1980s Mystras had to be supervised by her in-laws to make sure that she did not inadvertently transgress any local norms. Visiting outside kin circles was frowned on. If the husband's kin included a female sibling or cousin, the bride could consider herself lucky as this companionship enabled her to pay visits in the village or even in Sparta, to take the new baby out for walks and to cook special dishes together with the relative. Not many brides found themselves in this fortunate position, however, and the early years of marriage were largely passed, as one put it, '*kleismeni mesa*' – shut up inside. The recent innovation of town flat as dowry would prove a great improvement when attainable. The town offered a new wife more chance of companionship with other young people than a strange village did. And the preoccupation in villages with what other people might say – *ti tha pi o kosmos* – of a critical nature was somewhat mitigated by the larger population of the town.

Education

Most Mystriot girls stayed on at school up to the age of 18. (Schooling was only compulsory until 14.) The majority sat the university entrance exam, the *Panellinies*. Slightly fewer boys than girls took the exam, partly because they were less willing or able to endure so many years of rote learning – *papagalismos* (parroting); partly because they could find work where a degree or diploma was not required more easily than girls could. Unemployment amongst holders of degrees was high. A statistical study made in 1990 by OAED, the Manpower Employment Office, showed a 71 per cent increase in signed-up unemployed doctors and surgeons in the province of Attica for the period 1981–8; for primary school teachers the increase was 78 per cent. Despite the high rate of unemployment and the long years' wait for a permanent job, parents' ambition to have offspring with degrees showed no signs of abating.[4] Research by the Greek Statistical Service quoted in the magazine *Ena* on 11 September 1991 showed that half-a-million young Greeks held degrees; of these 50,000 had studied abroad. University entrance results in 1991 showed a continuation of the trend for more girls to pass than boys and for the greater proportion of successful candidates to come from the provinces.

Nearly all Mystriot candidates who failed the university entrance exam the first time re-sat it a year later, though two girls from returnee families moved abroad to study after failing once. Those who stayed spent the year in between attending crammers – *frontistiria*. On average, a parent paid out £55 a month per child for this coaching. And if the pupil succeeded in entering the university the parents would have to find the equivalent of a substantial dowry, about four million drachmas (*c*.£13,000), for the period of study. Tuition was free, but food and lodging in the university town had to be paid for. The likelihood of having a relation in Athens with whom to lodge was greater than in another town, but only those achieving the highest grades in the entrance exam could enter Athens University.

When a candidate failed two years running, strenuous efforts were made by the parents to find connections, *meson*, to engineer a public sector post. Up until four or five years earlier a girl who failed on all these counts had to sit at home until a suitable marriage could be arranged. By the mid-1980s most young women were allowed by their parents to try to obtain work in Sparta. Opportunities were very limited; there were jobs in the private clinics, radiographers, chemists and non-government offices. But even these could only be procured with an intermediary, usually kin or fictive kin. Employers took into account that young female employees were simply waiting to get married, lived 'free' at home and expected to earn no more than pocket money for clothes and bus fares. Such jobs had no long-term career prospects. However, an important aspect of this underpaid work, more often than not informal work without social insurance, was that as well as allowing the girl to get out of the house it provided her with the opportunity to be 'sighted' by a potential husband.

All the marriages of Mystriot girls that took place in the five years up to 1990 resulted in the couple living in Sparta, Athens or the USA. Sparta was now more likely to be preferred to Athens, and one Mystriot girl who married a man in the fire service in 1990 insisted that he get a transfer to Sparta from Athens (he came from a mountain village in the Taygetos). She had a dowry flat in Sparta and disliked the prospect of pollution, overcrowding and expense which she anticipated in Athens. This preference for Sparta over Athens was a new development and significant as a possible forerunner of a future trend; one that might lead to the fulfilment of the previous government's (Pasok) stated objective: 'the demographic (if not economic) reconstruction of the provinces'. Another couple who married at this time turned down a rent-free house two kilometres outside Sparta in favour of smaller and more expensive accommodation in the centre of the town. This husband was also a fireman and his stated reason for preferring Sparta was that he did not want to be seen in his fireman's uniform as he travelled to and from Sparta by bus. The motive for not being seen in uniform was the same as that which lies behind growing an exaggeratedly long nail on the little finger of the right hand to indicate that you are a white-collar worker.

Preoccupation with appearances was prominent both in Sparta and the nearby villages. A Mystriot woman going to Sparta even for a dentist's appointment would dress in her best clothes. A friend explained why: 'It's because in Sparta you will meet people who know you. It doesn't matter what you wear in Athens because there no one knows who you are.' Worrying about 'what people will say' – *ti tha pi o kosmos* – or 'how things should be done' – *kathosprepismos* – reflected the fear of ridicule which was so pervasive in these villages. A feeling of inferiority arising from their social origins may have lain behind this slavish conformity to Spartan fashion and perhaps accounted for their circumspect, incurious response to visitors to the village. A government-appointed crafts teacher who gave a fortnightly class for a year in Mystras and several similar villages was astonished never to be invited in, not even for coffee, while she waited for her bus, which in one village involved a three-hour wait. She attributed this lack of interest and hospitality to the wealth in these villages. She herself came from a poorer village in the north of Greece, where, as she told me, people were very open and welcoming. But perhaps Mystriots' stand-offishness stemmed rather from insecurity than from a sense of superiority. Avoiding contact with outsiders and not asking questions may have been due to fear of displaying ignorance or making fools of themselves.

A young woman from Mystras who had attended Patras University and taught maths at secondary schools in and around Sparta for several years introduced me to an Athenian colleague also teaching in Sparta. The Athenian girl, a sociology teacher, put on a play with a group of her pupils. The Mystras girl was admiring and said to me: 'You know, I who am a villager, *horiatissa*, would not know how to do such a thing, for as a villager I am not *kalliermeni*, cultivated/cultured.' Her observation was more an indictment of the education system than of the village;

an education system that, despite the virtue of being very accessible, stresses formalism at the expense of teaching pupils how to think. But her belief that the cause of her inadequacy was being a villager echoed the popular view.

Fear of what people might say seriously inhibited innovation and originality.[5] A returnee from New York wrote to his mother and sister in Mystras to say that his new wife would be shipping the furniture for their newly built house to the village. The sister at once telephoned New York begging him to do no such thing: the furniture must be bought in Greece with the advice of herself and her mother. The possibility that the American furniture might be superior in quality or design was immaterial. There could be no question of risking the family's social standing in the village with furniture that did not conform to Mystriot standards. That was in 1981; I saw the house in 1986 arranged to conform to local priorities. The result was of interest because it successfully embodied the Mystriot ideal. The impression had been created of a very formal city flat with heavy reproduction furniture and voluminous dark curtains kept closed. Most of the younger returnees' houses shared some of these features, though none had been quite as successful in creating the citified atmosphere. Villagers who had never left the village had not gone to these lengths but they had jettisoned a number of rural features in the 1970s when improved economic circumstances permitted alterations. One of the first features to go was the open fireplace, *tzaki*, associated with poor village houses. Ceramic roof tiles were replaced with modern flat concrete roofs, wooden balconies with concrete and metal. A shift in urban tastes in the 1980s dealt a blow to these modernising villagers when rusticity came into fashion and open fireplaces, ceramic tiled roofs and pine balconies became de rigueur. Unfortunately rusticity's new fashionableness did not improve Mystriots' self-esteem. They rightly suspected that the fashion, as in the aphorism, 'There is a vogue for peasant handicrafts but not for peasant attitudes,'[6] was limited to rustic products and did not include rustics or their way of life. So the struggle to demonstrate urban-ness continued and parents aimed to educate their children for white-collar jobs.

Education's urban image

In Chapter 1 we saw the ease with which a rural migrant in nineteenth-century Greece could with sufficient education qualify for a civil service job in Athens. Easy absorption into the urban middle class led to the establishment of an ideology, *astifilia*, which saw jobs in the state sector as the kind most worth aspiring to. This was a major reason for villagers to educate their children out of the village, reinforcing the association between city, education and social standing and perpetuating the image of village inferiority. The commonest insult hurled by angry city drivers at each other was *Apo horio eisai?* – are you from a village (that you're so incompetent)? While the highest recommendation a villager could make was: He's educated, *einai morfomenos*. Of himself the villager might comment self-deprecatingly: I don't know letters, *den ksero grammata*, not meaning that he was literally illiterate, but that he had had very little education. The city image which attached to educated persons extended to their dress and behaviour, preconceptions which led to great astonishment when confounded by educated foreigners. A campsite owner's wife was amazed that middle-aged backpackers staying at the camp turned out to be university lecturers. She expected lecturers to wear suits, carry suitcases and stay in hotels. A Mystriot woman who let rooms was no less astonished when a professor of biological sciences from the University of Aix-en-Provence lit the wood stove in her restaurant one cold April morning. *Kathiyitis!* (professor), she kept exclaiming after I had translated his card to her, 'and knows how to light wood stoves!'

Until the mid-1980s most aspiring villagers had aimed to base their careers in Athens, but now there was a trend for professionals to return to work in or around Sparta. The Mystriots who had left for Athens in the 1950s and 1960s were mostly from richer families; several of these had become lawyers or doctors, the leading professions in terms of social standing. Those that I met in the 1980s from this group belonged to a well-off elite in Athens, their success certainly contributing to the continuing association between education and prestige. By the 1970s, engineering had become popular; there were now two Mystriots in their mid-thirties practising as civil engineers in Sparta while a more numerous but less prestigious group had become teachers. Most of these taught maths and physics largely thanks to measures taken by the Junta to remedy the national shortage in this field. One consequence was an over-production of maths teachers, with many having to wait for years before getting a permanent position. Indeed, many had given up and opened a *frontistirio*, cramming establishment, in the nearest town.

Ironically, the latest profession to become popular was *geoponos* – agronomist/agricultural adviser. The popularity of this profession reflected the strengthening of the agricultural sector and the role played by EEC support. The Agricultural Advisory Board in Sparta, as we saw, was notorious for overmanning, corruption and inefficiency, but for Mystriots and Spartans *advising* a farmer was acceptable whereas farming itself was not. The British agricultural consultants I met were scornful of these bureaucrats, who with very few exceptions avoided fields and mud and cared very little about the practicalities of farming.

The new trend for professionals to return to the provinces after completing their studies was significant. It was a response to the deterioration in Athens' employment situation, the city's overstrained facilities, worsening pollution and quality of life. This shift in attitude did not, unfortunately, reflect a corresponding improvement in the provincial labour market, as the 300 or so cramming establishments in Sparta, run for the most part by out-of-work graduates, testified. At the same time, it could be expected to have a beneficial effect on the villages, both because the presence of educated villagers might contribute new ideas to the running of local affairs and because their presence might dispel the image of inferiority so long attached to the village.

In the mid-1980s, however, receptivity to new ideas was not to the fore. The presence in Mystras of educated younger villagers had not progressed beyond the stage of sowing dissension between the generations. If conflict was going to be the herald of social change as discussed at the start of the chapter, this was the moment. Signs of tension first arose with the establishment of the *Politistikos Syllogos*, Cultural Association, in 1981. The idea behind these associations, first established in the 1970s, was that young people (aged 18–32) in villages should initiate cultural activities for the edification of the local population. Government funds would be available to subsidise, for example, the hiring of a touring theatre group. The associations mostly limited themselves to organising the Lent carnival events and a fundraising dance or two. In Mystras the association met opposition at an early stage due to its mixed membership. Members met in a room allocated to them in the *Koinotita* (village council) building and, even if the members' parents themselves knew that these meetings were harmless, there were plenty of other villagers ready to say that improper activities were occurring. Although secondary schools in Sparta had been coeducational for over a decade, there had been no mixing of the sexes in public spaces in the village. In addition to their fear of gossip, parents began to find other reasons for objecting to the association. Their daughters were now spending too much time talking to other girls, exchanging home visits – a new phenomenon – when they should have been at home with their *kentimata*, embroidery (usually tapestry by numbers), or learning to cook special dishes. Clearly more than one aspect of the established order was felt to be under threat here. The growing resistance to needlework and domestic duties suggested that the girls had other plans than early marriage. More and more girls were in fact hoping to work after marriage and fewer were interested in early marriage. This was reflected in the increasingly later marriage age, late twenties to early thirties for women, and mid- to late thirties for men, a trend throughout Greece.

Despite initial doubts, the dances and carnival activities which took place in the first year were very popular and generally approved. By the second year, hostility had grown on the part of the elders, partly because they feared their offspring were the butt of local criticism and malicious gossip, partly because the young's activities were said to be becoming political. The carnival float that year called for the banning of cruise missiles, whereupon the right-wing mayor accused the association of having Communist affiliations. In the year of the national elections the ecology float, decked in green, was banned from the procession by the elders because its colour constituted political propaganda, green being the colour of the Greek Socialist Party. Suspicion of left-wing politics was endemic in this area, where, as noted, Civil War fighting between partisans and right-wing supporters had led to much bloodshed and bitterness. Many left-wing supporters had in fact left the village after the war. Opposition on the part of the older villagers probably resulted as much from fear of losing power in village affairs, and jealousy at the success of the association's activities, as from a genuine belief that the events were political. Subsequent events indeed showed that the association was actually believed to be conservative (New Democracy) in its affiliations.

In 1986 I gave a questionnaire to the members (all under 35) of the Cultural Association. What changes would they like to see in the village? Their first wish was development – *axiopoiisi* (αξιοποιηση) – of Old Mystras, that greater local recognition should be accorded its cultural and commercial potential. As a site of Byzantine art of exceptional beauty and quality it could become a centre for exhibitions of Byzantine culture. Such initiatives could lead to local appreciation of the site's value beyond its equivocally viewed role as supplier of sinecure jobs to those with good political connections. To date, efforts to launch such initiatives had been regularly thwarted by bureaucratic obstructionism on the part of the Archaeological Authorities themselves. The same obstructionist response defeated the new young mayor's efforts to get lavatories installed for the use of tourists at the site; at the end of the 1980s there were still none and the lower entrance gate was still closed so that walkers had to go another kilometre to the higher entrance.[7]

Similarly unappreciated was the association's programme of village improvement, which included installing a drinking fountain, new signposts and litter baskets paid for with funds raised at the dances. Inevitably these projects ran into trouble. Who should mend the water fountain when it broke, who should empty the litter baskets? The association was not offering a maintenance service with their donations though probably they should have. The unemptied baskets were removed by the *Koinotita*; the fountain stayed out of action.

Local village council elections were held in 1987. Three parties prepared to campaign: the Socialists (Pasok), the Conservatives (New Democracy) and the Independent Conservatives. Two of the three mayoral candidates were over 60; the incumbent mayor was 57. The existence of two conservative parties reflected the fact that both leaders wanted to be mayor. The rift threatened to give victory to the Socialists. Seeing the splits, the association decided to set up an apolitical party. They approached all the parties urging them to abandon their divisive campaigns and unite to support a party whose objectives were restricted to village improvement. After much debate the conservative parties agreed, doubtless to ensure a Socialist defeat. But they insisted that the association replace their mayoral candidate with another member of the association widely believed to be reliably New Democracy. The association duly won the election and installed itself in the *Koinotita* office. The community secretary, a permanent appointment and an important position as part controller of village bureaucracy, had held the post for ten years. She was the new mayor's aunt and undoubtedly one reason for his selection. As soon as the outgoing mayor realised that, contrary to expectations, his selected candidate would not be dictated to, he began to build up opposition in the village. This defined itself along age lines. Indeed some older Monarchists had voted for the Socialist candidate on the grounds that, being over 60, he would serve the village better than a young person. Before long the message that the village would regress, *paei piso*, for the next four years as a result of government by 'children' became increasingly vociferous. The new mayor was in fact 36 years old.

At the end of his term the former mayor had returned 1.5 million drachmas of the funds allotted by the Government for village projects. He had concluded that new projects risked losing local support, pleasing a few and antagonising many. The new mayor, by contrast, applied for and obtained generous funds to implement the various programmes he had in mind. These included locating a new water source, reforming the irrigation system, amalgamating the village school with two other villages to improve the pupil/teacher ratio, and organising a village garbage collection jointly with several other villages. This was a bold programme, especially insofar as it involved cooperating with other villages, a move understandably feared as a threat to village autonomy. The water and irrigation system reforms were eventually given up by the new mayor as generating more opposition than he could cope with.

The outgoing mayor believed that the legacy of the Civil War was partly responsible for the difficult relations amongst the older generation. A villager could still run into a man who had murdered his relations or whose relations he had murdered. It was alleged by older villagers that one effect of the eight years of Socialist government from 1981 to 1989 was the revival of the old political hatreds of the Civil War years. Perhaps the older generation simply felt ill at ease with democracy. The Mystriot who had been the Junta-appointed mayor from 1968 to 1974, and who by this time lived in Athens, told me in 1990 when the conservatives were back in power: 'Today everyone in Mystras loves one another (*einai agapimeni*), they're all right-wingers (*deksii*).' He was out of touch, but the assumption was that difference in political opinion precludes peaceful coexistence. That this was not so amongst the younger generation was demonstrated by the association's apolitical local government in which the members supporting the mayor were equally divided as regards political party affiliation.

During the eight years of Pasok government, political attitudes did change somewhat; not just because the importance of political clientelism for obtaining jobs where the labour market was so underdeveloped had guaranteed an increase in Socialist voters. Young people were increasingly united by their dislike of the non-meritocratic system, whereas older people resented not having a monopoly over local patrons. Moreover, Mystriot initiative was hampered by the powers of the Archaeological Authority, which affected village enterprises as well as access to jobs at the archaeological site.

The association members' attitudes had also been influenced by their very different experience. They had never worked in agriculture; they had attended school in Sparta and worked in Athens. The image of Athens was no longer the glamorised one with which their parents had grown up. While everybody was willing to take a sinecure job if the opportunity arose, these young people, unlike their parents, had no illusions about its intrinsic worth. A young person who failed to get into university would apply for a civil service job: 'It's a salary for a lifetime of sitting and doing nothing; I might as well try.' The civil service jobs were theoretically obtained by competitive examination, but everyone believed that most posts were allocated before the exams had taken place, that the exams were just a *vitrina*, a showcase. Amongst young people, at least amongst the more sophisticated, this state of affairs devalued the public sector and degraded the image of state employee, a very significant change in attitude. A young man on the village council who had failed to get a teaching job after graduating two years earlier was temporarily working at the archaeological site; his father had *meson*, influence. The young man found this embarrassing and was relieved when he found a job working for Sparta radio as a reporter. He was concerned about the poor reputation of state employment, to the point where he told me how pleased he was that his elder brother, till then a civil servant, had set up his own business in Athens.

One section of the population who did not fit the traditional pattern of urban aspiration consisted of the *teknites*, the artisans. There was a dearth of skilled workers in the area, an indication presumably of local distaste for all manual work, not just agricultural work. A Greek saying says the *teknitis* is first cousin to the *agrotis*, and artisans in Mystras enjoyed correspondingly low status. They were mostly from those families who had been the poorest in the 1950s, and what struck me was their self-respect and fundamentally different work ethic. Unlike the majority of the villagers they did show curiosity and did ask questions about the world beyond the village. At the time of fieldwork I attributed this difference in behaviour to their having no status to lose. Subsequently I attributed their outgoingness and curiosity to self-confidence; they were proud of their skills and whatever their social standing they were earning much more than an office worker. Moreover, by the nature of their jobs, which took them all over the province (as builder, carpenter or electrician), they were in control of their means of production and came into contact with a wider range of people than most Mystriots.

Innovation, as we saw with the *Politistikos Syllogos'* activities, was likely to encounter active obstruction from villagers. All kinds of success were resented if they took the form of new enterprises within the village, but resentment increased if the enterprises were agricultural. Someone else's success aroused jealousy whatever its nature, but if their success was not within the accepted framework of aspiration it was seen as threatening to local values. When a villager who had retired from working as a guard at the site opened a restaurant, his neighbours were not slow to accuse him of breaking the law in numerous respects: the kitchen was unhygienic; the souvlaki roasting annexe was on someone else's property; prices were not fixed; the noise level was unacceptable and customers were parking their cars illegally. For the first few months there were regular visits by the police summoned by neighbours. Gradually the protests died down and the villagers turned their attention to newer enterprises. A girl from Athens hired the ground floor of a house and opened a craft shop for summer tourists. As a single girl in her late twenties she violated every standard of proper behaviour; she was labelled as immoral and suspected in addition of drug dealing. While she was not spoken to by most of the villagers they eventually stopped trying to eject her. In both these cases, some degree of tolerance may have arisen when the villagers saw the very limited success that these enterprises enjoyed.

A much more negative reaction was displayed when a returnee had to leave New York because his wife suffered from asthma. He was in his late forties and had made a lot of money, enough to have built an apartment block in Athens. He and his wife considered living in Athens but decided that for her health and for the children's his village, Mystras, would be more suitable. He decided to buy land for an orange grove in the next village, Parori, in addition to cultivating his own land in the village and his wife's land in a village below. His wife's parents were originally from a mountain village, Agriani, in the Parnon mountains across the Spartan valley but had established themselves in their winter pasture village close to Sparta. This agricultural background influenced the wife's decision to farm together with her husband.

When the family first arrived in the village they set about rebuilding their house. Generally, returnees improved their houses and settled down to educate their children while very often the husband would commute to the States to continue earning. The same happened in this case. But on his return in the mid-1980s the husband settled down to farm. He bought a tractor and he and his wife were seen driving to their fields every day. At first the villagers were incredulous; to have enough money to live from rents and to choose to farm was strange. For a wife to farm as well after spending years in a city was unheard of. The women asked the wife why she had come back just to get dirty. She became embarrassed to go to church and started sending the children by themselves. After they had been back for two years, the catastrophic March snow and frost of 1987 killed all their young orange trees. There was much satisfaction on the part of the villagers; not, one hopes, out of *Schadenfreude* but because this catastrophe vindicated their negative views on agriculture. Locals often said that this area was not really suitable for agriculture; the land was too uneven, the climate too uncertain and the water inadequate. This was not the view of the specialists I knew at the Agricultural Bank. It was probably not believed by the villagers, but it justified them in their rejection of agriculture and seemed almost a cause for pride. Every time a maverick villager scored an agricultural success he or she was condemned, as in the case of the woman who installed a well with EEC subsidies. This was an exceptionally intelligent and enterprising woman in her early sixties whose children were both professionals in Athens. Having installed the well she was vilified as a Communist. In the case of the returnee family, it was widely assumed that the snow catastrophe would put an end to their agricultural activities. However, they replanted and hostility towards the family increased. A year or two later the whole family became Jehovah's Witnesses (the only ones in Mystras), thereby cutting themselves off from the village symbolically as well as professionally.

Initiatives that were an extension of a conventionally established resource such as restaurants and shops met with adverse criticism temporarily. Eventually they found their niche and the village realised that nothing much had changed; the smaller the success the less the opprobrium. Novel initiatives like that of the returnee dental technician who opened a campsite or the well-off returnee engaging in farming were resented as threatening established norms and the status quo.

Urban influence a retrograde force

On the basis of the ethnographic evidence I believe that the influence of *astifilia* as experienced by villages like Mystras and small towns like Sparta has been a retrograde force. The focus on higher education and civil service employment has resulted in the reproduction of earlier values and economic strategies that ignore political, social and economic changes. Conformism and fear of criticism constitute a serious brake on innovation. The prevalence of clientelism as the means for securing public sector jobs has been a disincentive to individual initiative, while the personalistic framework, which allows local authorities to block one enterprise while permitting a similar one, has further underlined the absence of 'modernity' in the Weberian sense of a rational calculable modus operandi. The effects of emigration have similarly been an obstacle to progress. Loss of a large portion of young people, émigrés' reluctance to sell their land thus preventing its redistribution, the fact that remittances or pensions from abroad and rents from urban property reduced the need and impetus for local enterprise, have all acted as disincentives to reform. For these reasons I argue that *astifilia* in conjunction with emigration has fostered economic stagnation and reduced productivity.

CHAPTER 4

KEFALA: BUCKING THE TREND

Kefala in the 1980s

After some months working in Mystras I discovered that while the surrounding Taygetos and Spartan plain villages shared many of Mystras' social and economic characteristics, there had been a different development across the Spartan valley in the foothills of the Parnon mountains. This socio-economic divergence dated back to at least the 1950s, when emigration from the Parnon villages had been very much lower than from the Taygetos. The figures were striking: 65–70 per cent of the Taygetos population had emigrated in the 1950s and 1960s; 30 per cent or fewer had emigrated from the Parnon, with the exception of one village, Skoura, discussed below. In contrast to the green-ness and fertility of the Taygetos villages, the Parnon terrain is drier, the west- and south-facing hills exposed to longer hours of sun and less rain than those in the shadow of the Taygetos range. Yet agriculture had been expanding since the 1950s, and all but the oldest farmers had now mechanised as far as possible. Local resources were exploited to the full, with olive cultivation, viniculture and livestock breeding constituting the chief sources of income. Those with less land trained as apprentices to a trade such as painter, plumber, tile layer or mechanic to supplement their income.

There was little in the ethnography to suggest the existence of communities in areas of small cultivators where emigration and the pull of the town had not substantially depleted the population. So I decided to expand my original research objective to make a comparative study of Mystras and a Parnon village in order to discover which factors might explain this divergent development. In the context of this book, which explores the causes of *astifilia* and its effects on the Greek economy, it proved particularly illuminating to look at an area where *astifilia* was absent. The differences highlight some of the socio-economic features which foster productivity and suggest an alternative trajectory which sees value in rural development.

Kefala (pop. *c.*350), the village I chose to study in the Parnon, lay 20 kilometres southeast of Sparta, at a height of 340 metres. While the terrain was very much drier than that of Mystras, villagers' properties were much larger. Was this the variable underlying low emigration and differential response to the 'pull' of urban aspiration? This explanation was refuted both by Kefala's past development and by the village of Skoura, five kilometres west of Kefala. Skoura was the exception in this area to the pattern of low emigration. Much of its land lies beside the river and is extremely fertile as a consequence. Yet during the 1950s and 1960s, 70 per cent of its population emigrated. By the late 1980s most of the few remaining young people worked or aimed to work in Sparta or Athens in public sector jobs. In several respects Skoura closely resembled Karpofora,[1] of which Aschenbrenner writes: 'Due to its mild climate, fertile soil, and a considerable area with irrigation, it has a richer agricultural potential than many villages.' Yet, he says: 'Even with farming advantages and a favourable, accessible location, Karpofora has followed the general pattern of other far less blessed villages. It too has suffered depopulation through out-migration of adults and the *current rejection of rural life by its youth* [...] people have chosen to leave village life even though two apparently primary motives are lacking, namely, agricultural impoverishment and lack of modern amenities.' (My italics.) Exactly the same could be said of Skoura, which likewise enjoyed better conditions than its neighbours in terms of agricultural assets.

When the earlier ethnographers considered the causes of rural exodus they emphasised the pull factors – the social cachet attached to working in Athens, the perceived inferiority of village life – endorsing my findings relating to the ideology of *astifilia*. However, the question of push factors was not examined and these need to be considered if one is to fully understand the factors involved in large-scale out-migration. Here it is helpful to look closely at a village's relations of production. A survey of those villages that like Mystras and Skoura had experienced very high levels of emigration revealed a pattern. (Excluded from this category are inaccessible mountain villages.) The villages were all fertile and well-watered and, in the period just before emigration, cultivation was of an intensive nature and population dense. Land distribution was unequal, with most of the land concentrated in the hands of one or two larger landowners. The remaining land was fragmented as a result of partible inheritance. Conditions for the majority who worked as sharecroppers were oppressive and exploitative. When the opportunity came in the 1950s to leave the village, a majority opted for exodus. Reading between the lines of Aschenbrenner's ethnography of Karpofora, there is evidence regarding the relations of production, both at the time of exodus and later, which suggests 'push' elements. The significance of the role played by relations of production was confirmed by a survey of those Parnon villages where emigration was lower. These had a history of less-intensive cultivation, with greater emphasis on the pastoral side of the economy. Share-herding terms were more favourable to the worker than sharecropping terms. They enabled the worker to accumulate wealth in the form of animals and eventually to own a herd and operate more independently of the landowner. The discovery that the surrounding *roumania* long seen as infertile scrubland was actually arable led newly independent herders to consider renting or buying land, especially when mechanisation became available thanks to newly accessible bank loans. The astifiliac villages, by contrast, even following an advantageous change in relations of production, continued to reject local opportunities in favour of public sector jobs. The view that engaging with agriculture was demeaning outweighed propitious local developments.

As well as different attitudes to village life and agriculture there were striking differences in age and gender relations between the two areas. Mystras, as related above, was still a patriarchal society. In Kefala relations between old and young and men and women were more egalitarian. According to the Greek folk model and the outdated modernisation theory that it echoes (modern equals urban, backward equals rural) one might have expected the reverse. The flaws in modernisation theory are long acknowledged, but the model in this case had a kind of visual plausibility that sustained it. The agricultural village of Kefala with non-asphalted roads, goats, sheep and chickens visible all over the village, *looked* more old-fashioned than the suburbanising Mystras; the relations within the social institutions were not on view. Mystriots, as we saw, were concerned to behave in as urban a way as possible, both with respect to employment and with respect to interior decoration, dress and manners. Disengagement from agriculture looked urban and hence modern according to the folk model. But one result was an increase in women's economic dependence and social isolation, leading to the perpetuation of patriarchal relations. If modernity entails responsiveness to change economically and socially, it was the Kefalai who were modern.

Background to Kefala

The Parnon mountains, highest point 1,935 metres, run from north to south, parallel to the Taygetos range across the Spartan plain.

The eastern face of the Parnon range drops precipitously down to the sea so that access is easier from the sea than overland, while the western face of the range is open and rolling. There is forestation above the 1,000-metre level, black pine and Greek fir, while much of the lower area is treeless scrubland reflecting the dryness of the region. The area has a long history of pastoralism, traditionally practised by transhumant herders, many of whom were *dyplokatiki* – two-village dwellers – who lived in their mountain village in summer, moving to the lower village in winter. The earliest birth registered for Kefala in the records every village has to keep for the purposes of military conscription, the *Mitroon Arrenon Stratoloyias* (register of males for army conscription), is 1816. The Venetian census of Grimani of 1680– 1710[2] shows six families as resident in Kefala, 24 people in all. The discrepancy may reflect the fact that Kefala was only the winter village for transhumants until the early nineteenth century, so the six families in the census may not have been permanent inhabitants.[3] The Kefalai believe that the village was established in the 1820s, when the revolutionary captains came down from the mountains to overthrow the Turks and establish Greece as an independent nation state. Until this time the area was in the hands of Turkish pashas for whom the locals worked as sharecroppers. The revolutionaries drove out the pashas, and two leading captains from the Mavromihalai and the Varvitsiotai families took over their lands, which included large areas close to the river Eurotas. Like the pashas the captains cultivated labour-intensive crops such as rice, lentils, maize and cotton, using local labour on a sharecropping basis.

The majority of Kefalai were originally from Agriani, a mountain village 20 kilometres northeast of Kefala at a height of 1,000 metres. They did not move down all at once but gradually over a period of almost 200 years. As well as thousands of sheep, about 40,000 in 1940, the inhabitants of Agriani (Agriniates) had an additional source of income from the pine forest, where the trees were suitable for resin tapping. The resin, transported in hides, was sold as preservative to wine producers all over the plains area. The shepherds also sold cheese, meat and animals for breeding. In addition to their legitimate activities the Agriniates had a reputation for animal stealing. Their mobility enabled them to keep an eye out both for rich winter pasture land and rich farmers with an eligible only daughter – *monahokori*. A shepherd's son might marry into such a family as an *esogambros*, a groom who marries into and lives with the bride's family. The groom would probably have a skill such as carpenter, roofer or painter – a source of income in the summers when olive cultivation work is minimal – while in peak work seasons he would work on his wife's family property. *Esogambri* can be disparaged as inferior,[4] but Agriniates had a reputation for hard work and cleverness as confirmed by a local rhyme: '*Giati na paro tin karekla edo otan iparhi Agriniatis me mialo*'. Why take the chair (stick of furniture) from here when there's an Agriniatis to be had with brains.

In Agriani villagers had vineyards and grew wheat, but families were large and gradually the population outgrew its capacity for supporting itself. More shepherds began to move down to their winter pasture areas on a permanent basis during the first half of the twentieth century.[5] In Kefala by the 1940s two-thirds of the villagers were from Agriani. Following the war, when the Marshall Plan led to several road-building projects locally, a number of Agriniatis bachelors came down to work on the road that was being constructed between Gkoritsa (east of Kefala) and Sparta. Several of these men married into Kefala, some as *esogambri*, others renting huts and living neo-locally in the village.

By the 1980s there were only a few people living permanently in Agriani, though half-a-dozen full-time shepherds continued to go to the village from May to October for summer pasture. Agriani shepherds' permanent base was now in their former winter pasture areas in the foothills villages. By the end of the 1980s there was no longer a school in Agriani and the shops and village council only operated in the summer months. But the villagers who had moved away were still very attached to their birthplace, dwelling on its delicious water and its healthy climate. Many would spend part of the summer in the village or send the children with grandparents to escape from the heat and mosquitoes below, and everyone attended Agriani's summer festival.

Earlier relations of production in Kefala

Up until the 1950s it is possible to identify three social strata. At the top there were the two big landowning families, the Mavromihalai and the Varvitsiotai. Neither of these families lived in Kefala but they owned large tracts of land on either side of it. The Varvitsiotai were based in Skoura but took over a large tract of land to the north of Kefala known since Mycenaean times as Melathria, evicting in the process the three families who lived there. The Mavromihalai owned much of the land to the south in the region close to the Eurotas river known as the Piri. Both these families included members who were at one time or other Members of Parliament. Their revolutionary history meant that initially they were quite different from the big landowners in Mystras who had been tax collectors – *kotsabasides* – under Turkish rule, getting rich by overtaxing the poor and pocketing the surplus. Both the Mavromihalai and the Varvitsiotai were an important source of patronage to their employees, but not a source looked back on with warmth: 'They helped you out in times of illness or crisis as long as you put a cross by their candidate's name at election time, but there was no question of them helping you or yours to move away in case of need,' it is recalled. Villagers' recollections of the shop owners and itinerant merchants were similarly negative. It was not the humble villagers who were seeking to procure patronage through asymmetrical godparent or marriage-sponsor relations, they claim, but the greedy merchants offering sponsorship in order to extend their clientele.

The second-highest social stratum consisted of the richer village families. As well as owning larger properties than the rest of the villagers, each of these families also owned an olive press. While these families could not offer patronage on the scale of the estate owners, they employed favourites in the village on a sharecropping basis, helping them out when they got ill or into debt and confiscating their land if they proved unable to pay their debts. They are recalled with much greater rancour than the estate owners because, it is said, they were stingier employers than the Varvitsiotis family. This was probably true since they operated on a much smaller scale and their profits depended on maximising exploitation – they needed labour not votes.

The lowest stratum consisted of the rest of the villagers. Nearly all the Kefalai up until World War II were shepherds. They owned almost no olive trees, and cultivation was limited to extensive grain crops with some wine and honey production. (In the 1940s it is estimated that there were at least 1,000 beehives around the village.) Most of the villagers' oil came from sharecropping on the Varvitsiotis estate. Olive work on the estate was either paid in cash or in exchange for olives for oil, in which case the worker took 20 per cent of the olives they picked. Grain was grown on the estate's fields; the grower gave the estate owner a third of the grain harvest (*to trito*) and kept the rest for himself. A villager in his eighties in 1988 recalled the time before and during the war when over half the village looked after the estate owner's animals, sheep, goats and cows. The basis of the share-herding terms, he explained, was this: the contract was for seven years; the first year the herder took one young animal to every seven taken by the estate owner; the second year, two; the third year, three; until in the seventh year the flock was divided in half – *to misthoma* – half to the herder, half to the owner. At this point the contract could be brought to an end. The milk and the wool were equally divided between herder and owner throughout the period. These terms enabled a villager to build up a herd of his own relatively quickly.

Having established his own herd he might leave the flock to be herded by his children, or work only intermittently as a sharecropper, sending his wife and children to the estate while he took charge of the herd. A villager who made sufficient money from his animals to invest in some land gradually shifted from pastoralism to cultivation. There was plenty of land to be bought cheaply, particularly in an area just southwest of the village. It was cheap because as related above it was generally believed to be infertile and suitable only for grazing. It was *'roumania'*, scrubland, which before the days of bulldozers required back-breaking work to turn it into arable land. In the 1930s much of the land that was not *roumania* was used by the villagers for small-scale grain cultivation and vineyards. Some villagers in the 1980s still had vineyards in this area whose 'white' soil is well suited to viniculture.

The availability of land in the 1950s, albeit, before mechanisation, very labour-intensive to prepare for cultivation, provided an opportunity for the Kefalai to free themselves from their harsh and exacting employers without leaving the area. This was the situation when transatlantic emigration in the 1950s became possible. Emigration in Kefala began in 1956 when 15 villagers emigrated to Australia. A few more emigrated in the 1960s to Australia, Canada and the USA. In the late 1950s and the first half of the 1960s those Kefalai who left were mostly young men chosen by lot from amongst their brothers. A little later some young women followed to live with relations already abroad or to arranged marriages; these young women came from the poorest families. A small number of Kefalai moved to Athens. In the village of Skoura, very large numbers of villagers were taking advantage of this opportunity to leave. Their work conditions were harsher than those of the Kefalai since the riverside lands were very intensively cultivated and their employers, the Varvitsiotai, lived in the village. In contrast to Skoura the other villages in this area lost no more than 30 per cent of their population and from two villages of herdsmen, Hrisafa and Zarafona, exodus was even lower. In the case of Gkoritsa, a larger village immediately to the east of Kefala, emigration abroad was also smaller. Gkoritsa had experienced an earlier wave of migration at the beginning of the twentieth century to Egypt. Some of these migrants had returned with fortunes; one family endowed the village of Gkoritsa with a middle-level school, *skolarhio*, an important source of accessible education for the Gkoritsiotes. Another built a sanatorium in Sparta for tuberculosis sufferers (which is now the hospital); another endowed one of the first secondary schools in Sparta. But education did not lead to significant exodus and farming continued to flourish.

In Kefala two immediate consequences of exodus despite its small scale were fewer family members to take care of the flocks and land cultivation and fewer available villagers to work for the richer villagers and the Varvitsiotai. However, by this time oxen had largely been replaced by mules and donkeys, a change that reduced the burden on family labour somewhat since while oxen had to be taken to graze and watched, donkeys and mules could be tethered and left. More importantly, donkeys and mules as beasts of burden reduced the labour involved in transporting water for planting, brushwood for fuel, sacks of corn or olives. From the 1960s onwards, loans for machinery as well as for land purchase were obtainable from the Agricultural Bank. In the early 1960s two villagers in their twenties bought tractors (second-hand), the first in the village. Their example was soon followed; ploughs harnessed to tractors enabled villagers to plough much larger areas in a shorter time, while transport of tools or produce to and from the fields was much easier. As a result, more villagers started planting olive trees, calculating that olive cultivation would produce the highest and most stable return for labour. Olive cultivation began to expand in the 1960s and 1970s; it was less labour-intensive than vines or grain, particularly with the advent of mechanisation in the 1960s. By the mid-1970s more villagers cultivated olives and fewer were full-time shepherds. At the same time, there was an increase in home-based small-scale breeding of goats and sheep, the number fluctuating according to season. These were raised both for domestic consumption and for sale of their milk and meat to itinerant merchants.

Relations between the villagers and their employers changed radically. The majority of the richer families failed to mechanise so that by the 1980s when labour costs had risen and fewer villagers were available to work for them, these landowners had sold or rented most of their property to the villagers. Much of the land sold was uncultivated grazing land with a few wild olive trees on it. The buyer would hire a bulldozer to break up the scrub and then plant olive trees, grafting the wild olives with cuttings from cultivated trees. All these changes – the replacement of animals by machinery, the shift from shepherding to olive cultivation, the introduction of small-scale animal breeding, the availability of bank loans and the sale of most of the Varvitsiotis estate – meant that by the end of the 1980s most villagers were able to work sufficient land to make a living without additional employment. A family with less land might work on another villager's more extensive land for a daily wage – a *merokamato* – once their own farm work was completed, or hire themselves out seasonally in another village. A villager with a skill such as a painter or roofer would increase his income by working in the summer when field work was minimal.

A second fundamental change could be seen in the division of labour and the role of women. Before the introduction of machinery much of the heavier work was done by women. Transportation of goods to and from the fields, digging of holes for planting the olive trees, grain harvesting, domestic chores such as water fetching, had all been women's work. In the past the men were more likely to take charge of the flocks, often at some distance from the village, leaving the women to work on the estate or on the family's land. With much of the work now mechanised, with water piped to the houses, women in the 1980s had fewer heavy tasks. They were now more equal partners in the family enterprise. They were in charge of small-scale animal breeding and the income that this produced; they were indispensable for the olive harvest and they were co-workers at tree-pruning time. They worked in the vineyards at grape-picking time – the *trygos* – and helped with the fodder and grain harvests. Their vital economic role was fully recognised, the more so since most marriages were endogamous and wives were also inheritors of village land.

Kefala in the 1980s had 78 inhabited houses and about 350 inhabitants. A large proportion of the population was under 40. Sixty families, mostly those from younger households, owned a tractor while the majority of the elderly couples living on their own (most of whom were former bigger landowners whose offspring had left the village) still used a donkey and a mule for agricultural work. Altogether the villagers farmed about 7,000 stremmata (700 hectares, *c.*1,750 acres; 1 stremma = 0.1 hectare). The average size of property per household was between 80 and 100 stremmata, excluding most of the elderly households whose properties averaged about 30 stremmata since many had sold off much of their land. The land was officially classified by the government as 'semi-mountainous', a status which entitled it to higher farm subsidies than 'plains' land, and lower subsidies than 'mountainous' land. A further 2,000 stremmata were rented elsewhere, chiefly in Skoura where the scale of emigration had left a depleted population, many of whom were elderly returnees. These river-watered lands were ideal for fodder cultivation such as clover, vetch, maize and grass. The Kefalai also rented absent or inactive Skoura owners' olive groves, for which they paid rent in the form of a small quantity of oil.

Land in Kefala was largely frost-free; most properties faced south and west; temperatures in winter averaged 5°C at night, 10–15°C in the daytime; summer temperatures from 20°C at night to 36°C in the daytime. Kefala's most serious natural drawback in the 1980s was lack of water. Rainfall was largely limited to the winter months, and groundwater had become scarcer, partly as a result of increased use, partly following three years of drought at the end of the 1980s. There were 15 privately owned wells in addition to the communal water source from which water was first piped to village houses in 1965. After 1986 this source had dried up by the end of June each year. A new source of water was finally located five kilometres below the village, just outside Skoura, and the programme to bring drinking water to the village was completed in the autumn of 1989. The water had to be pumped up to Kefala so that water costs doubled and the average household's water bill rose to 12,000 drachmas (c.£40) a year. In addition to this domestic water source, the mayor of the time initiated a scheme for field irrigation.

Olives

The main crop in the 1980s was the oil olive; Kefala had about 80,000 trees. In addition, there were 8,000 trees of kalamon – *harakolies* – table olive trees. Oil olive trees were almost all cultivated (*imera*) olive trees, many the result of grafting wild olives. Unlike wild olive trees, 'tame' or cultivated trees require watering for the first two years. Kalamon trees require more water, are vulnerable to frost (though if the olives are damaged they can still be used for oil) and are more troublesome to harvest since the olives must be picked selectively as they become ripe. However, kalamon trees became increasingly popular as the income per kilo was higher and the olives would be sold direct to the merchant. Oil olives have to be pressed before being sold, which involves paying the press owner and possibly an extended wait until the oil is sold. The division of most properties into an average of five parcels as a result of inheritance or endowment enabled the farmer to choose where to plant which type of tree for optimal results. In the 1980s the average annual production of oil per household was four tons (averaged over two years since olive trees produce highly every other year). Some households produced as much as ten tons; one or two as little as two; but the majority's average was four. Four tons brought an annual income of 2,800,000 drachmas (c.£9,330) including the EEC subsidy.[6]

Livestock

Second in importance in terms of income were livestock. Each household had between ten and twenty animals depending on the time of year (five to nine goats, two to five kids, four to six lambs). All households raised hens and rabbits. Taking an average of ten animals per household, a clear profit from meat sales was reckoned by villagers as 150,000 drachmas annually; milk sales brought in a further 100,000 drachmas. This income was supplemented by the household's 'free' consumption of meat, cheese, milk and yoghurt, a very substantial saving given the cost of these items on the market: lamb at 1,000 drachmas per kilo; kid at 800 drachmas per kilo; sheep's milk at 80 drachmas a kilo, goat's milk at 70 drachmas a kilo. Except when there were drought conditions compelling the farmer to buy fodder from elsewhere, the availability of almost free fodder-growing land in Skoura greatly reduced outgoings and was a major promoter of villagers' engagement in livestock breeding. The costs involved (e.g. threshing costs: 11 per cent grain taken by the itinerant threshing machine owner plus 110 drachmas charge per bale) in growing an average of eight stremmata of barley, four stremmata of vetch, clover and grass, plus some maize, were covered by the sale of straw from the barley and wheat crop to the cow owners in the villages just outside Sparta. The unevenness of the terrain precluded the use of combine harvesters, so harvesting was by hand with sickles. A touring threshing machine was hired and spent several days at a spot just outside Kefala to which the villagers transported their harvested crops.

The trouble involved in animal breeding and the fodder production side of it reflected the Kefalais' concern with 'quality', a preoccupation that happily coincided with a growing preference on the part of the Greek public for hormone-free, ecologically respectable 'green' food. Thus there was a good market for animals fed on 'home-grown' fodder as opposed to artificial feeds, which were said to make the meat smell fishy, and Kefala meat was much in demand amongst the itinerant merchants who paid correspondingly higher prices per kilo. Villagers preferred the best quality for their own consumption too, even if it cost more in time and money. For example, 28 families grew hard wheat despite the fact that the hilly terrain precluded the use of machines and three days had to be spent on the average eight or nine-stremmata field by two or three people harvesting with sickles. And even though hard wheat was subsidised by the EEC (4,000 drachmas per stremma) it was still cheaper to buy ready-milled flour. For the staples *hilopites* and *trahanas* – types of pasta – as well as for bread, which each household baked fortnightly in brushwood ovens, home-grown wheat was preferred for its superior quality. Every household had a kitchen garden, *perivoli*, and those owning a well could produce vegetables even in the summer months. The rest had to buy from the itinerant greengrocers based further south where there was abundant water and a flourishing greenhouse industry.

Viniculture

Thirty-five families had vineyards in the 1980s, the rest having destroyed their vines at an earlier stage when olive trees first became obviously profitable. At that time many villagers had tried planting olive trees amongst the vines for lack of alternative space but this led to the dehydration of the olive trees and the vineyards were dug up. Since vines are more susceptible to disease than olive trees and more vulnerable to weather conditions this was a logical solution given the lack of alternative planting space at the time. In the 1980s there was a renewed interest in viniculture as a commercial venture. Two men planted ten stremmata of vines, one adopting the foreign system of planting in rows using wires to support the plants, with sufficient space between to plough. Previously vines had been planted like cabbages, making it difficult to get at the individual plants for thinning and spraying. Ten stremmata produced an annual income of 1,000,000 drachmas (c.£,3000) and, thanks to the village's past reputation for high-quality wine, there was a ready-made market, with clients coming from all over this part of the province.

Maximisation

The readiness to diversify income sources was both a way to minimise loss if one source should fail and a way to maximise use of family labour since olive cultivation only required intensive labour for three months of the year. One stremma of olive trees required 38 hours' work a year, 70 per cent of which was harvesting, with the average property size of 80–100 stremmata requiring at least three pickers for three months. If the farmer was not to lose money (daily wages started at 4,000 drachmas per seven-hour day) he had to use family labour. Every supplementary activity using family labour was a bonus. Two frequent responses to my questions about activities such as animal breeding and fodder production were, 'We've nothing else to do with our time', or 'You don't reckon your labour' (*den ipoloyizis tin doulia sou*) – family labour was not 'valorised'.[7]

The household

The majority of houses consisted of two storeys, the lower inhabited by the older couple, the upper inhabited, or to be inhabited, by the younger couple and their children. A number of upper storeys had been completed though the sons of the house had not yet married. Most of these house improvements were made in 1981 and 1985, when national elections were held and easy loans were part of the electoral campaigns. Families with more than one son usually aimed to build a second house in the yard or nearby. Wives brought a dowry of fields, and in some cases money, but not a house; at least 85 per cent of village marriages were endogamous, resulting in the consolidation of village land. Until the late 1980s, marriage age was early so that the majority of joint households contained two sets of able-bodied adults. Apart from the ploughing, which was always done by a man on his own, and the harvest, which required all available members of the family, work in the fields since the introduction of mechanisation was done in husband–wife couples. This applied to work in the vineyards, sowing of grain, spreading of fertiliser, pruning and burning the olive tree branches. Other jobs such as milking and feeding the domestic animals were usually shared by a couple, though the greater responsibility for the animals lay with the woman, usually the elder woman in the household as long as she was fit. But these arrangements were flexible and varied according to circumstances and the stage reached in the domestic cycle of the household. Within the household the division of labour varied. If there were young children at home, one of the women would have to be with them. A majority observed that in the fields you can see what you have achieved, whereas in the house cleaning and cooking means monotony and repetition and your mind focuses only on worries, *stenohoria*.

Labour exchange, *allilovoithia*, was common and in summer the pasta staples for the household were made by groups of women who took it in turns to assemble at each other's houses for the purpose. Similar work parties gathered to prepare the traditional cakes and sweetmeats before a wedding. Grape harvesting was always done with a group of friends and relatives of both sexes. Since many families no longer had vineyards the pickers could choose choice bunches of grapes to take home in exchange for their labour. The purpose of these work parties was to harvest the grapes fast in congenial company. The grain harvest was also done in groups, in this case as an exchange, since the work was arduous. Grain harvesters' work was recompensed with a hot meal brought out to the fields or eaten at the grain owner's house at the end of the day, while grape harvesters were given a cold picnic in the vineyard. If a helper did not cultivate grain himself, some other work would be exchanged; the grain field owner might look after the helper's flock several times during the year. Formerly, when grain was grown very extensively, harvest help was paid. The principle in the 1980s that determined whether non-exchange help was paid or not was: where the crop is a cash crop you pay helpers; where it is for domestic consumption you do not. Quite a lot of mutual aid went on between villagers on a casual basis.

As long as there were two active men in a household, the younger was more likely to go and work for a wage in the off-peak season, while the elder did farm jobs such as olive tree pruning, woodcutting, hauling of branches from mulberry or olive trees for animal fodder and farm maintenance jobs. The young men ploughed for elderly households for a wage, harvested their olives once their own harvesting was finished, and in summer took jobs in Sparta as drivers, waiters or working for the forestry commission, which hires extra firefighters for the summer. In the summer of 1991 following a poor olive harvest caused by drought, middle-aged men as well as young men sought work, working for example in local cement works, or in one case in a potato-peeling business supplying the military base near Sparta. A number of men in the village regularly worked in secondary jobs. Those who were skilled workers worked all over the province in the summer months. A total of 140 days' non-agricultural work was allowed without forfeiting agricultural status and the benefits that went with it such as farm subsidies, pension and healthcare. Middle-aged fathers tended to spend more time working on their properties than their sons, partly because they 'found' work to do. The young men who did wage work in other people's fields noted, however: 'You never feel the pleasure in cultivating another's (*ksenos*) field that you get when you cultivate your own.' The system of property transmission encouraged such feelings since family land was normally divided when offspring reached their early twenties. Early transfer ensured that the heirs took an interest and that a young man could innovate if he wanted to. Importantly, it made the young landowner eligible for farm subsidies and improvement schemes.

In the late 1980s a farmer with two sons and a daughter who was slightly lame asked his daughter if she would prefer her inheritance in the form of land or as a down payment for a flat in Sparta. Her lameness meant she was not strong enough to do strenuous farm work and was therefore unlikely to find a farmer husband. Hence her father thought she might prefer to live in Sparta where at the time she was working in an office. She chose land because, as she explained, the land planted with olives would produce an income while the down payment on a flat in Sparta would have to be added to 'and anyhow nothing would induce me to live in Sparta'. Preference for land over real estate or money was the more usual choice in this area. A young man who married a girl (a *monahokori*) from Gkoritsa rejected his father's advice to ask for the dowry in money instead of land. The father argued that the five-kilometre trip over to Gkoritsa made the land impractical. The son pointed out that the income from the olive oil on the land would be more valuable than dowry money, which would not buy so large a property in Kefala.

Enterprise

In the 1980s Kefala and Krokaies, a village further south, shared the distinction of having borrowed more from the Agricultural Bank than any other village in the province. In Kefala the catalyst for development had been the sale of the Varvitsiotis estate, which meant that with the help of government loans villagers could acquire more land. In Krokaies the catalyst was the discovery of an abundant water source. The high level of borrowing reflected dynamic and expanding economies rather than oppressive indebtedness; indeed, sources from the Agricultural Bank confirmed that most Kefalai had a high level of savings deposited.

The villagers' response to the freak weather conditions of March 1987, which cost them the following year's olive harvest, illustrated their flexibility and readiness to adapt to new circumstances. Every household doubled the number of its animals and used the time that would have been spent harvesting to take the animals to graze, thereby saving on fodder. When women or girls took the animals to graze they took along their knitting because, as they said: 'Out in the fields we know we'll get three or four hours' uninterrupted sweater-making time.' Several families planted market crops, such as beans, which they sold in Sparta. Some of the younger men found jobs in Sparta, one as a driver for the post office; two opened a video shop. The mayor got a job collecting milk from some villages to the north for a cheese-making factory. Two families took on flocks; men with building skills found building jobs (or painting or tile-laying) further south. A number of villagers – men, women and teenagers – went to villages further south which had escaped the snow, and picked oranges. Some of the ventures misfired. One man who bought 30 lambs to sell for Easter meat sales had to sell them early on; they required more expertise (as he ruefully acknowledged) than he had reckoned and kept getting ill. One of the partners in the video shop disliked working in Sparta and gave up. But everyone increased their efforts in one direction or another as well as tightening their belts. The increased leisure was not wasted either; chess playing became a major pastime.

Experiments

A couple of years after the end of a disastrous drought period the then mayor installed irrigation on a plot of land at the edge of the village and set up a market garden. He calculated that the villagers, having little to do in the summer months, would be happy to pick the produce to be sold, in exchange for taking home some vegetables for themselves. As anticipated, villagers gathered for the early morning session picking tomatoes, aubergines, peppers and melons, in the same spirit as for a grape-harvesting session. Different villagers continued to come right through the season. However, growing vegetables of acceptable shape and form for the market turned out to be much more trouble than it was worth given that there were easier alternatives, and the mayor admitted that he would not be doing it again.

The same readiness to experiment could be seen with regard to tools. In 1989 itinerant sellers went through the villages selling olive-stripping machines. The machines could be had on trial for several days and most households tried them out. They calculated that the machines increased the amount of olives picked by nearly a third, significantly reducing the number of days needed for harvesting. The disadvantage was that to be used efficiently they required an extra pair of hands. The obvious solution here was exchange of labour between families, not uncommon between friends anyhow. However, a new disadvantage was noted when pickers realised that the machine made too much noise for easy conversation. 'But the only reason we pick together is for the talk,' one family complained and did not invest in a machine. Despite these problems, 30 families did buy a machine (which cost 150,000 drachmas (£500) each).

The combination of limited labour and extensive land challenged the farmers to find ways to maximise productivity within these constraints. Innovators were welcomed as pioneers of new initiatives whose outcome would determine whether to follow suit or not; a quite different scenario from that in Mystras where a 'limited good', zero-sum game outlook prevailed, in which new initiatives were feared as threatening existing incomes and/or posing a danger to the status quo. Ways to improve income included: increasing mechanisation so as to reduce labour time and enable expansion of properties; investment in new irrigation schemes to increase olive trees' productivity; the introduction of new crops such as the kalamon table olive, which sold at a higher price than olive oil; experimenting in the case of livestock farmers with different fodders and new breeds of sheep or goats. Because the farmers did not 'valorise' their own labour they could maximise their work and time input without cost. At the same time a clear distinction was made between being *ergatikos* (hardworking), a quality which evoked admiration, and being *pleonektis* (*pleonexia* = cupidity), a quality denoting antisocial tendencies such as avarice.[8] There was a view that once needs had been fulfilled, drudgery should be limited.[9] If not, the farmer was criticised as greedy, accumulating beyond his needs, endangering his health and his social relationships. What he already owned had to be managed and maintained of course but if he kept acquiring more and more land, crops or animals, then he was criticised for loss of judgement, for being a slave to accumulation.

CHAPTER 5

SOCIAL RELATIONS IN KEFALA

The attitude towards village life and agriculture in Kefala was shaped as explained by developments arising from the original relations of production, one consequence of which was much lower out-migration. The farmer's position as a self-employed entrepreneur with access to land independently of political influence meant that he could act autonomously. Innovation was not resented because if proved successful it showed the way to less enterprising farmers and at no cost to the innovator. The first man to introduce a new system for planting vines was followed by others when they saw its practical benefits. The shepherd who introduced a new breed of sheep to the village was proud when shepherds from his and other Parnon villages followed his example. Given these circumstances there was less cause for distrust and secretiveness, recurrent themes in many of the ethnographic accounts. Aschenbrenner, for example, observes that there is a pronounced tendency for a family 'to be secretive and guarded about its affairs [...] a submerged, ultimate mistrust of those outside the family'.[1] In Kefala the lack of competition for resources doubtless helped to reduce the jealousy – *zilia* – prevalent in many studies of Greek rural life. Negative self-interest – *symferonda* – another theme central to the ethnographic discussions on interpersonal relations, was less prominent as a result. This is not to say that rivalries and jealousies were absent in other spheres, rather that they were minimal in the agricultural sphere and hence did not put a brake on productivity or cooperation. Moreover, the advantages of reciprocal help at harvest times made good social relations expedient.

Gender relations

Significant changes in gender relations had occurred over the two decades prior to my fieldwork in 1988 as a result of changing relations of production in Kefala. The marked age–gender hierarchy present in Mystras and noted in other village ethnographies reflected a traditional association between agricultural society and patriarchy. Aschenbrenner summarised the Karpoforans' views as follows: 'What comes out finally is that males do tend to be strong and females weak. In the context of their different natures, males are superior and females are inferior. Flowing directly from such a view is the traditional deference and obedience women are expected to show to men.'[2] Ethnographers such as Friedl, Aschenbrenner, Dubisch and du Boulay, while recording these kinds of attitudes, are at pains to suggest that appearances are deceiving. To support the view that women are not as disadvantaged as might appear Aschenbrenner quotes du Boulay:

> the Greek understanding places women at the centre of the life force contained within the family, and this position, while it does not give women any form of crude authority or power in the world in which physical strength operates, nevertheless provides them – and their men also – with an inalienable sense of their own value. [This] provides them with an abiding strength in the face of adversity, and enables them to stand up to instances of ill treatment from their men with an unshakeable knowledge of their own essential dignity.[3]

A sense of dignity hardly seems adequate compensation for the situation described. A similar attempt to identify mitigating factors and hidden power is made by Friedl in an article 'Appearance and Reality':

'It must be clearly understood that formal authority even about household and farm management rests with the husband and father [...] But to say that women have informal power over household economic decisions and over the economic and marital future of their sons and daughters is not a trivial statement [...] the family is the significant unit of social and economic structure in the Greek village community, and therefore power within that unit must have important consequences for power distribution in Greek society as a whole [...] There is another sense in which women have power in Vasilika. This does not operate in affecting decisions or actions affirmatively. It is a check upon the power of men through women's ability to disrupt orderly relationships in the men's world. Insofar as men's honour depends on the behaviour of their womenfolk, these women exercise a real measure of control over them. It is the women's willingness to behave chastely, modestly, and becomingly that is a prime necessity for the maintenance of men's self-esteem.'[4]

It would be difficult to find more convincing evidence for women's inequality than this account of 'weapons of the weak'. That the situation for women in Kefala had been something like that described in the ethnography can be gathered from a number of sources, chiefly older women's own accounts of domination and exploitation by husbands, mothers-in-law and fathers. The celebration in the past of men's name days but not women's was another indication of earlier male dominance. A 24-year-old girl recalled at the end of the 1980s that she had not been allowed to ride a bicycle as a child, this being considered improper for girls. 'But I was rebellious (*epanastatiki*) and rode one anyhow; now it's normal for girls to ride bicycles.' Likewise, in the past, girls and schoolchildren of both sexes were punished if seen in the square. But by the 1980s it had become normal on warm evenings for women and girls to meet there, and by the end of the decade mixed groups of young men and women and children regularly gathered in the square. This was in marked contrast both to Mystras and to Glendi, the community studied by Herzfeld in Crete. Herzfeld writes of Glendi:

> This spatial arrangement [of the square] dramatizes the symbolic contrast between male and female stereotypes in Glendiot society [...] The square is a public space, and as such is controlled by male conventions [...] Other, mostly young, women line the wall on the 'female' side, watching the general activity but avoiding direct personal contact with individual young men. To a very large extent the women of Glendi, much as their counterparts elsewhere in rural Greece, are typecast as passive, indecisive, and unable to control either their sexuality or their tempers [...][5]

Gkoritsa, five kilometres to the east, was often cited by younger Kefalai as more progressive than Kefala. In Gkoritsa men and women had been mixing freely for much longer: there were women on the village council; there was a women's association; women went without embarrassment to sit in the village cafes; husbands and wives often went together to a village cafe in the evening. The Kefalai attributed what they saw as this more enlightened spirit to the earlier presence of the middle school in the village: 'It's education, *morphosi*, that makes people progressive,' they said. By the late 1980s, when I was living in Kefala, I was struck by how little sexual division of leisure there was: couples of all ages were frequently to be seen together during their free time. In the past, older women recalled, men would more likely spend their leisure time drinking at the tavernas and it was not unusual for wives to be beaten by husbands who had drunk too much. Women had very little leisure time in any case; until 1968 the village was without electricity or piped water, and women's domestic tasks included fetching household water from the common source half-a-kilometre below the village in addition to all their other duties.

A number of factors contributed to the demise of patriarchal relations in Kefala. The acquisition of tractors made both men and women's work in agriculture less exhausting physically. The installation in every house of electricity and piped water reduced domestic tasks very substantially. Whereas education for most villagers over 50 had ended after a few years of primary school, the shift in crops and cultivation methods now freed older children from some of the agricultural work. Furthermore, the new road financed by the Junta was close to the village, and for the first time Kefalai had access to a bus service so that school pupils no longer had to stay with relatives in Sparta during the week but could come home each day. This led to an increased number of children attending school, and by the 1980s most villagers in their late twenties had attended secondary school up to the age of 15, with many going on to three years of *lykeo*. As a result, young people's numeracy and literacy were usually of a higher standard than that of their parents. During their secondary school years they came into contact with a greater variety of backgrounds and opinions, so it was easier for this younger generation to deal with bureaucrats, with the new ideas coming over the media and with practical matters such as form-filling. A crucial difference between these pupils and those from urban-aspiring villages was that education was utilised for the benefit of farming rather than rural exodus. A husband might recognise that his wife's scholastic skills were superior to his; accounting, for example, had become a highly estimated skill. The olive press manager told me that he relied on

103

his wife to manage the paperwork, which he found confusing. A wife's inherited land, her labour and her skills were even more valued now that farmers were self-employed as opposed to being sharecroppers, as couples were joint partners in the farming enterprise.

Preference for endogamous marriage

In contrast to marriage patterns across the Spartan valley, where exogamy was the norm, Parnonites preferred endogamous marriage – marriage within the community. One reason for this preference was no doubt practical since the bride's dowry would be land within the village area. By contrast, the rationale in the astifiliac villages for choosing exogamous marriage was in part to extend social networks and increase the range of connections for jobs or political influence.[6] Young women in Kefala believed that marrying into another village would be isolating and, in the absence of family support, might lead to loss of independence. Customarily a bride who married outside her village brought a dowry in cash rather than in land, a fact which Kefala girls saw as further endangering a bride's autonomy. The intensive contact I observed in the late 1980s in Kefala between wives and their mothers and siblings underlined the value attached to staying close to one's birthplace. Continuing to live in the village where you had grown up and gone to school meant that you were familiar with the landscape and the spatial layout as well as with all the inhabitants. A shop or cafe in Kefala was a centre where you met your relations and your former schoolfriends; not as in Mystras an unfamiliar place where, if you ventured there at all, you were stared at by semi-strangers. These factors contributed I believe to the self-assurance which was so noticeable in Parnon village women and such a contrast to the behaviour of women in the astifiliac villages.

There was a great deal of village group socialising in Kefala. Dances were frequently held in the village square, attended by young and old. Village-organised expeditions by bus to places of interest were always oversubscribed. Whenever the primary school put on a play or recitation everyone attended. The school's Parent–Teacher Association held a supper and dance in the village square at the end of the school year, which the whole village attended, young and old. The large proportion of young people in Kefala contributed to the lively atmosphere at these events, which were further enlivened by the exhibitionist dancing of several middle-aged dancers whose exuberance and talent were a regular source of admiration and amusement. The day after one such event I heard one mother observe: 'It was a perfect evening; nicer than the feast day celebrations when people from other villages come – no rowdiness, more a family affair (*oikoyeniaka*).' She was right, the atmosphere had been one of comfortable intimacy and almost everyone there was indeed related.

The fact that every household in Kefala shared a similar work routine determined by the seasons, facing the same risks and uncertainties of weather, no doubt added to this solidarity. An example of cooperation and community discipline was the summer fire watch. Every summer, fires in Greece destroy acres of forest. In the 1980s, fires in the Peloponnese had destroyed acres of olive groves as well as forest. Several villages had had three-quarters or more of their trees, their chief source of income, destroyed. Some villages installed a fire watch following a scare, but very few kept it up as a regular routine throughout the summer months. Kefala set up a system with the volunteers allocated in order of the alphabetically arranged electoral roll. Where a villager was reluctant he was not forced to comply but he faced opprobrium from the majority who were naturally intolerant of 'free riders'. Few villagers did make difficulties. Keith Legg in his book *Politics in Modern Greece* writes of Greeks: 'When community efforts are found, they can usually be attributed to an obvious congruence of public and private interest.'[7] The comment is intended as a criticism of Greeks' low level of community cooperation. This is surely to miss the essence of the problem, which all over the world is precisely getting people to recognise the congruence between private and public interest, to comprehend that a cooperative effort will benefit individuals as well. With regard to fire watching, Kefalai had seen the link as demonstrated in this example of civic conscience in action. A telephone call for help to put out a fire came from a village some 20 kilometres to the northwest. The callers knew that the Kefalai owned water tanks attachable to their tractors and this was an SOS for urgent help. Within 15 minutes of the call I watched 60 tractors plus tanks filing out of Kefala; an army could not have organised itself more quickly. On this occasion Kefalai reached the scene of the fire only to find access blocked by 'sightseers'. The police stood by helplessly until the Kefalai arrived and ordered those blocking the road to get out of the way. This time, despite outside help, the village lost almost all its olive trees. Following this tragedy, churches throughout the province took collections to pay for animal fodder so that the villagers who had lost the income from their olive oil would not lose their livestock as well. The Kefalai donated generously, well able to imagine the terrible impact; as one young farmer's wife moved by the catastrophe put it: 'It's as if they were your children, the wretched/ burnt trees.' (*San na itan ta paidia sou, ta kaimena dendra.*)

Interpersonal relations

Openness was perhaps the most striking characteristic both as regards behaviour and the actual layout of the village. Spatially Kefala is like an amphitheatre, with the houses ranged down the hillside, enabling villagers to follow the movements of other households from all over the village. Socially, open communication was recognised as positive; unburdening oneself of worries and emotions however transitory was seen as therapeutic. When a wife from the neighbouring village of Hrisafa committed suicide aged 48 she was especially pitied because her husband rarely allowed her to visit neighbours; 'and how can one bear one's worries unless one tells them to others?'

Making a fool of oneself, so dreaded both in Mystras and in the village studies, was much less of a problem in Kefala, perhaps because nearly everyone was related. Villagers exposed themselves to mockery almost willingly, the fondness for laughter allowing both for unconventional behaviour and for overreaching oneself. The workaholic farmer who took on 30 lambs the year the olive crop failed and had to sell them at a loss for lack of expertise was, as we saw, quite open about his failure, making no face-saving excuses and joining in the laughter when mocked. Potentially scandalous behaviour was positively relished, as on the occasion when three middle-aged men repaired to the graveyard to sing dirges (*miroloyes*) one moonlit night after midnight. The escapade was met with indulgent laughter by their fellow villagers.

Village fire watchers posted at the chapel of Prophet Ilias one August night gathered some friends and organised a feast of octopus and prawn (fasting foods) – it was the period of abstinence preceding the Dormition of the Virgin. The party lasted with music and singing throughout the night and was the subject of much amusement in the village the next day. Acceptance of non-conformity meant that individuals could behave eccentrically and established institutions mocked without the perpetrators being censored. At Apokries (Carnival) a group of men and women, young and old, all masked, enacted a funeral procession that took in the whole village, ending in a mock funeral service outside the main church and concluding in farce as the dead body rose from the coffin.

A factor contributing to the marked spirit of fun in Kefala was undoubtedly the age distribution which was weighted towards the young. An effect of this was the forming of horizontal groups that counteracted the family group and any tendency the older generation might have had to exercise patriarchal domination. The early devolution of property from father to son was another factor. The interaction between the younger age groups also had a salutary effect on interpersonal relations. The older young men – married and single – were looked up to by the teenage boys. So when a boy rode his un-silenced motor bike up and down the village continuously despite householders' protests, it was the young men who got him to desist, not through assertion of authority, but through reasoning.

That the mayor was elected at the age of 23 was a further indication that youth was regarded positively in Kefala; more especially since the mayor did not represent the majority politically and (an only child) had comparatively few relations in the village.[8] A majority of voters in Kefala reasoned that this man who was ten years younger than the rival candidate was better qualified to be mayor. He had completed *lykeo*, served as an officer during his military service, was unmarried and would therefore be able to devote more time to the village's affairs. Moreover, the rival was considered to be out for himself. In discussions about village social relations the mayor stressed the importance of this age distribution, observing that the younger villagers were more flexible, more receptive to new ideas. The older generation allowed the young to take the larger responsibility for managing village affairs partly because they believed that the young's educational advantages fitted them better for this role in village government; partly perhaps because they themselves were more absorbed by agricultural concerns. A former mayor who had been in office in his forties told me: 'Thanasis is better at being mayor than I was because he "knows letters" better than I do and being unmarried does the work the day it comes in.' This man was in fact exceptionally energetic and intelligent, one of a succession of very able mayors. The fact that Kefalai were less dependent on patronage meant that their choice of mayor could be based on the

individual's ability to manage village affairs rather than on his
political connections.

Conclusion

The way Kefalai managed their affairs in the 1980s demonstrates
that clientelism and repudiation of village life are not endemic to
Greek society. The history of how local relations of production
have influenced the village's development highlights the link
between low emigration and social conditions favourable for
economic productivity. From this example we can see that there
are alternatives in Greece to *astifilia* and the clientelist modus
vivendi which have contributed so perniciously to the country's
economic situation.

CHAPTER 6

PROVINCIAL CHANGES FROM THE 1990s: STAGNATION VERSUS PROSPERITY

When the Maastricht Treaty, leading to the creation of the euro, was signed in 1991, Greece was very far from meeting the convergence criteria. Indeed the *Financial Times* had reported in December 1990 that the European Commission was insisting that Greece make a ten-per cent cut in public sector staffing by 1993, a cut which would entail the loss of at least 65,000 jobs.[1] The treaty stipulated that its members must limit debt to 60 per cent of gross domestic product (GDP), with annual deficits no greater than three per cent of GDP. Greece's annual deficit was 11.5 per cent of GDP and its inflation rate was 19.8 per cent (compared with the EU average of 4.07 per cent). But once again, as in 1981 when Greece achieved formal accession to the European Economic Community, rule-bending geopolitical preoccupations took precedence over economic considerations and Greece was admitted to the monetary union. In 1991 it was hoped therefore that the stringent conditions being imposed by the EEC on Greece as the member with the lowest productivity rate and record budget deficit would prove the catalyst for reform.

Already in the 1980s, Aschenbrenner's Karpoforans had noted that, 'Due to inflation, the real income of salaried positions such as those of police, teacher, bank employee, and civil servant had fallen severely.' Furthermore they were having increasing difficulty 'finding white-collar positions, even after meeting the escalating education requirements'.[2] In these circumstances, given the obstacles to emigration and growing shortage of public sector openings, I hypothesised once again that astifiliac villagers in the 1990s might be galvanised into looking for new income-generating strategies, perhaps even in agriculture. In Mystras the continuing presence of more educated young people reflected their disillusion with Athens and might well inject long-lasting dynamism into village life. The generation in their twenties and thirties, increasingly critical of clientelism, was looking to 1992 as the year when Greece's greater exposure through EEC policies to Western bureaucracy would initiate a new era. Their optimism was misplaced as we now know, but their belief that an impartial clientelist-free, legal—bureaucratic framework was a prerequisite for progress was promising. It seemed likely that as the generation in their sixties lost their stranglehold on village politics and social life these attitudes amongst the returning younger generation would lead to more innovation and local initiatives.

The new *Koinotita* (village council)'s latest activities, as we saw in Chapter 2, indicated a commitment towards village improvement that their predecessors had lacked. In a bid for reforms, a council member had written an article in a Sparta daily newspaper in 1990 drawing attention to the poor service offered to tourists at the Byzantine site. Despite an entrance fee, the writer observed, there were no public lavatories on the site; furthermore, the site closed at three o'clock each day thus compelling those tourists who could not arrive at eight in the morning to walk round it during the hottest hours of the day. Worse, there was only one drinking water tap available to the public on this site, which takes several hours to view and involves steep terrain. Eventually, two improvements to the site did occur: the opening hours were extended and a public toilet was installed at one of the entrances. Also the council's bid for the management by Mystriots of the government-owned Xenia restaurant was successful.[3]

However, the hoped-for increase in village dynamism did not materialise. By the end of the 1990s the biggest demographic changes to the village were the loss of young people to Sparta and the arrival of workers from former Communist countries. Albanians and Romanians moved into some of the more derelict Mystriot houses, which had been left empty for decades by transatlantic emigrants. The immigrants found work in construction all over the province. In Mystras they worked restoring houses, some of which belonged to Athens-based Mystriots reviving their village roots, while in the 2000s a few houses were bought by non-local entrepreneurs hoping to attract tourists with traditional-style guest houses. The immigrants also worked in the increasingly neglected olive and orange groves. Female foreign workers found work caring for the elderly, who were now in the majority following the move by most of the young to Sparta. These carers, mostly Romanian and Russian, provided a much needed solution both in Sparta and the villages to the problems arising from Greece's budget deficit, which had depleted staff numbers at state hospitals and old people's homes.

In 1999 Greece was rejected as a Eurozone member for failing to meet the EU's economic criteria. In 2000, however, it was decided that if the deficit could be reduced to an acceptable percentage of GDP, the country could after all join the currency union in 2001. This despite its having one of the highest inflation rates in Europe. To qualify for membership, the Greek government must ('but seriously this time', one imagines the EU admonishing) adopt a tough austerity programme, making deep cuts in public spending. So we have now seen the European authorities' rules bent in 1981, 1991 and 2001. In 2002 the euro started circulating, replacing the drachma. A year or two later

I noticed that the traditional slang nomenclature had not changed when referring to the new denominations. The word *taliro* formerly used to denote a five-drachma piece now referred to a five-euro note, blurring the fact that the latter was worth far more. The common complaint that prices were rounded up and that the change of currency had made things more expensive may have been true, but calling the new currency by old misleading names was a slippery slope, especially dangerous in the 2000s when banks were ringing people to offer loans of €1,000 without requiring collateral.

'Mystras is dead; nothing ever gets off the ground,' lamented one elderly Mystriot in 2013. She was the enterprising woman who had succeeded in getting public funding for the watering system for her orange grove in the 1980s. 'Look at the abandoned Sassendas project and the illegal buildings still standing unfinished decades later. Look at the uncultivated *baxedes* (orange groves). Look how unsupervised unskilled foreign workers have pruned the olive trees; it will take years to get the trees producing properly again.' She could of course have reflected that as her own children were professionals living and working in Athens her own family had not helped to stabilise the population.

The man who in contrast to most Mystriots had been active in agriculture as well as having a restaurant in the 1980s reported on the village's situation in 2015: 'The bell keeps tolling as the old die and the young leave. *Mikrainei to xorio* – the village is getting smaller; young couples prefer to live in Sparta.' Asked about tourism he replied: 'Tourists don't come into the village much. There might be busloads at the *Archaia* (the Byzantine site) but after visiting they leave for the islands.' On the subject of the new subsidies to help people become farmers he pointed out that only the under-forties were eligible, which ruled out most Mystriots. Up until the recent elections his son had been vice mayor in Sparta where he and his children lived. Might the grandchildren work on their Mystras property? I asked. 'You know, the generation of grandchildren if they didn't learn together with their fathers on the job don't know how to work. Seems as if education beyond a certain age creates a generation of people who don't know how to work and who don't want to,' he replied.

Sparta

In 2011 the effects of the economic crisis were just beginning to be felt in Sparta. By the end of 2012 a friend who works in a Sparta bakery noticed that, 'This year at the time of the Christmas/New Year festivities people were buying less than half of what they bought last year. And now people no longer buy whole loaves without thinking.' By 2014 a young professional chef who cooks for marriage and baptism receptions said there was much less work now that everyone was economising and gatherings were being limited to fewer and fewer guests. Shops with 'to let' or 'for sale' signs had been multiplying since 2011 and dozens of small businesses continued to close down. The Church-run Voithia sto Spiti – Help in the House – which helps people living within a five-kilometre radius of Sparta was being applied to by increasing numbers for support. On a visit to their office in 2014, I saw, in addition to locally donated dry goods and yesterday's bread donated by bakeries, aid packages of food sent by the EU. It struck me as a bit ironic that the EU was giving aid at the same time as imposing austerity. Much more ironic, said the priest in charge, is that before austerity they were giving us twice as much.

Kefala

The influx of foreign labour from nearby former Communist countries from 1990 onwards had a very significant impact on the economies of the agriculturally active villages in the Parnon. The availability of cheap seasonal labour to cover the intensive olive-harvesting period enabled villagers to take on larger landholdings (bought or rented). New developments in harvesting tools and machinery reduced the time needed to strip the trees, thus also limiting the period for which hired workers were required. In the 1980s the olive harvest had lasted until March; now harvesting was finished by the end of January. In Kefala a boost to the trees' productivity came from the introduction of drip irrigation after a new water source had been located. The extra expenditure involved initially deterred some from irrigating, but the increase in the watered trees' productivity was soon evident and most found it worthwhile to invest. Such improvements were encouraged and facilitated by two advisers from the Agricultural Bank, both of whom were exceptional examples of agronomists at once engaged in helping villagers and expert in their field. The loans which villagers were able to obtain at very low cost (two-per cent interest rate) over these years made possible both the expansion of landholdings and the establishment of the new irrigation infrastructure.

In the period 1995–6 a few villagers decided to move to organic farming. Not everyone was interested in making the move, partly because they were sceptical as to the advantages, but also because they were reluctant to incur the initial expense involved in switching to organic fertiliser and spray. However, as in the case of drip irrigation, when they saw the pioneers' success on the market, the other villagers followed suit.

In 1998 a group of villagers established an organic olive oil business, a commercial company jointly owned by its stakeholding members as distinct from a one-man business, which set out to export oil and olives without using middlemen. Each member had to contribute to the infrastructure and maintenance costs of the company and to bear losses should some years be less profitable. The middlemen who had been buying the village's oil and kalamon (large eating) olives tried to discourage this enterprise, which would deprive them of a valuable source of organic produce for which there was a thriving market. But the founding group members, by marketing proactively at home and more especially abroad, quickly established a core of customers in the USA and Germany and, up until the imposition of Western sanctions, in Russia. Over 50 per cent of the produce (oil and kalamon olives) is sold abroad. New markets are being explored and the company continues to be profitable. In order to meet demand (since over half the villagers take their produce elsewhere) the company supplements its members' kalamon olives by buying in from non-member organic producers in neighbouring villages. From a highland village across the Spartan valley in the Taygetos it buys in olives whose oil has a distinctive taste much favoured by some foreign clients. As part of its marketing strategy the company organises periodic visits to Kefala to give foreign clients an insight into the whole production process from tree cultivation to harvest to the pressing. These visits have led to an increase in foreign orders.

The villager who after some years took over the business from the founder has to work very hard with his team to keep abreast of the day-to-day running and marketing while continuing to work his own land. As he once put it, 'The work is killing but I love the challenge and I'd rather overwork than hang out in the *magazi* (shop/cafe) listening to guys talking about their tractors.' Not everyone, however, has been a contented member of the company. Some have left, claiming that they are not receiving their fair share of the profits or that the company is selling at too low a price. One family took the company head to court accusing him of embezzlement. Despite the fact that all members have access to the accounts which record income and outgoings, this family maintained that there is no financial transparency. They made a point of employing an Athenian lawyer as most likely to win their case but lost. Another family who thought they could make a bigger profit on their own subsequently regretted leaving. One or two members have been asked to leave. Villagers who are not members of the oil company do not believe that it is profitable.

The company works on the basis of long-term gains; members have not only jointly invested in the infrastructure and building of the enterprise, they must continue to invest in its upkeep and marketing. Understandably some villagers would prefer to take their produce elsewhere, have it processed and take their money without being involved in the responsibilities, risks and complexities of membership, whatever the profits in the long run. Or, as one villager who runs his own restaurant business said frankly, 'I don't want to be in an organisation where decision-making is shared; I have to be sole boss or not be involved at all.' He sells his kalamon olives to the highest-bidding itinerant merchant and takes his oil olives to a press in another village. Like the oil company he is looking for the most profitable outcome, but from his own business. He is a good example of village entrepreneurship. In the 1980s and earlier, the village shops and two cafe-restaurants had been in the lower part of the village near or in the central square where the church is. But as the owners of these establishments either retired or, in the case of the shops, stocked less and less, the brothers recognised an opportunity. In the 1980s their family had been poor, owning very little land, and the brothers had worked for other people at harvest time while earning in summer as waiters and delivery boys in Sparta. With their savings they eventually acquired fields of their own and in 2005, a time when the banks were still lending, they took out a loan and built a small grocery shop and cafeteria on a plot they owned halfway up the village. The elder brother, the driving force behind this enterprise, calculated that in winter people would do their shopping at the grocery store as no one has time to go to Sparta at harvest time, while in summer when they have time to spare he reckoned that villagers would make more use of the cafe-restaurant. He could charge less for coffees and food than in Sparta, having no rent to pay, and villagers would save on petrol costs by staying in the village. His calculations proved accurate and the restaurant drew people from other villages as well. An appealing extra was access to the internet, and the brothers took the time to teach foreign workers how to use it.

Difficulties arising from lack of trust like those experienced by the olive company have arisen in other fields of business. There are half-a-dozen shepherds in the village, some of whom have olive groves or stakes in family-owned groves as well as flocks of sheep or goats. Their main source of income is milk, which they sell direct to a cheese-making factory. But in the case of one shepherd a fifth of his income comes from meat, which he has to sell to a middleman. To bypass the middleman he had hoped to open a butcher's shop in Sparta, but the capital necessary for acquiring premises was not forthcoming as banks had stopped lending. So he approached two shepherding associations in Lakonia proposing that they should jointly open a shop in Sparta. Initial interest faded when it came to putting the plan into practice, largely due to the same difficulty experienced by the olive oil company – lack of trust between the would-be joint partners – but also, he suspected, because most shepherds being considerably older were more conservative in outlook. At 43 he is the youngest shepherd in the province.

A shift in crop production has been taking place since 2010, with much more emphasis on growing kalamon olives, which are more profitable to grow than oil olives. As well as planting kalamon olive trees in preference to oil olives, some villagers started grafting their oil olive trees with kalamon until, as some in the village observed, 'At this rate they won't even have oil left for the house.' This was a significant point in a country that consumes annually per capita 17.9 kilograms of olive oil[4] (though consumption in towns has fallen over the crisis years). Despite these reservations, more and more villagers have continued to switch as not only is the price for kalamon olives higher, they can be sold as soon as they have been picked.

Future prospects and the 'crisis'

Villagers agree that the years from 1995 to 2010 were particularly good for farmers. Most continue to be optimistic about the future despite the uncertainties arising from the crisis; as one declared, 'Crises open up opportunities.' Another maintained initially at least that 'The crisis has shaken people up into mending their ways and new reforms will lead to a smaller and more efficient bureaucracy.' While these farmers did not suffer a fall in income between 2010 and 2016, the crisis has spurred them to look even more proactively for new ways to generate income. One woman I know regularly searches the internet for information on crop diversification and new candidates for subsidies. Different plants and trees are being tried out, some because they come with government subsidies such as pomegranate trees and *frangosika* (prickly pear), others such as rosemary and oregano because there is more demand than ready supply. One villager tried cultivating a breed of wheat containing less gluten which he had seen growing in Arta in the north of Greece. Unfortunately a virulent weed grew in between the wheat that did not respond to organic spray, and the project had to be abandoned. Now someone plans to experiment with a new kind of fig to grow on the *roumania* (scrubland) at the top of the village. Before the crisis, villagers who owned land here were considering a plan to advertise plots for sale to foreigners looking to build holiday houses; the prize of a free plot to go to the first taker.

One might have expected that unemployed Spartans, whose numbers have grown very considerably since the onset of the crisis, would come and work in these villages at harvest time. Villagers would prefer to hire Greek workers as they come without the risks or bureaucratic complications attached to hiring foreign workers and without the need for accommodation. But efforts at recruiting local unemployed have not yet been successful; the jobless young seem happy to stay at home albeit out of pocket. Whether this is due to the view that such work is considered *ypotimitiko* (demeaning) or simply more trouble than it is worth is not clear. The younger Kefalai by contrast hire themselves out to other villages once their own harvesting is finished.

Although the Kefalai themselves were not suffering economically they were very exercised by the political situation from 2012 onwards. Each time there was an election – two in 2012, local and Euro elections in 2013, an election and a referendum in 2015 – they were very engaged and there was much discussion as to where the country was heading. Initially they had hoped that the reforms to the bureaucracy proposed by the troika would reduce corruption – use of *meson* (connections) and/or *mizes* (bribes) – and result in fewer but more competent bureaucrats. One of the reforms involved sacking those unqualified bureaucrats who had got jobs through connections or on the basis of falsified documents. The farmers' struggles with the Department of Agriculture in Sparta were a long-standing cause of anger and resentment towards the department's staff: 'They keep you waiting while they chat on the telephone or eat. They tell you to come back again and again, each time with a different document, and it's not just a show of power, often they themselves don't know the procedures. Remember how many got in through the back door either with fake papers or with *meson*.'

Corruption, however, continued to flourish, with some inspectors ready to take bribes in every situation, whether complicit in a claimant's exaggeration of trees lost after a fire, or ready to reduce the amount of tax a citizen owed in exchange for a backhander. The whole system was undermined as the honest citizen lost out while the liar made good, engendering distrust and resentment at the injustice and encouraging deception. Despite the notices on the walls in Sparta's hospital forbidding the handing over of *fakelakia* – little envelopes (containing money) – most doctors still expect to be given sweeteners and demand them if not proffered. A villager who applied to install solar panels in a field he owns beside a road was informed by the authority that this road was too narrow for the purpose. He was then approached by someone in charge of the list of applicants and told that in exchange for €5,000 his request could not only be granted but he could be placed third on the list. 'Not interested,' the villager responded in disgust. On an everyday low-key level of corruption an article bought in a shop often has two prices – one with, one without a receipt.

In 2014 a number of villagers were lamenting the troika's failure to institute right from the start an electronic system for taxation, billing and receipts, replacing the endless accumulation of paper receipts which had simply fostered confusion and more corruption. 'You can judge how entrenched the rottenness in the system is,' said one villager, 'by the persistence of *pelatismos* (clientelism); *voulevtes* (MPs) still exchange jobs and favours for votes; bureaucrats still deny us the documents we need in the hopes that we'll bribe them.' 'And we go along with the corruption,' added another. 'When a government inspector comes to a business owner and says, "Tell you what, if you give me €2,000 I won't ask for your receipts for the year and we'll consider the inspection complete," does the owner refuse the offer?' Several villagers agreed: 'Even if it means becoming a protectorate and never mind under whom – Germans, Great Britain, US, whoever – we have got to break away from the old rotten system; we need clear laws which last for a decade rather than as at present changing from day to day.' Others took a different view: 'The EU only brought us into the euro system so as to control us; now they're going to take us over and we'll lose everything. The Germans want to buy up our country for themselves.'

There was more unanimity before the 2015 referendum when villagers agreed that:

> Whatever the election produces not much will change for us
> in this village because we have our fields, our animals, our

vegetables and fruit whether we're in the euro or not. We would prefer to stay in the euro but drachma or euro we will be all right, while those in towns are screwed, even looking in the *skoupidia* (rubbish) for food to eat. Those who went to work in the public sector because they thought that shepherding and agriculture were only for the stupid have problems today; they're losing their jobs or their salaries are falling fast and they can't make ends meet.

In the same vein a woman in her nineties indicating a field she owned below her house said: 'It used to belong to a woman who married a man from Skoura; the family moved to Athens to *piastei sto dimosio* (latch on to the public sector). Those people who left farming to latch on to the state! What would people eat if there were no farmers? *hartia* (documents)?' Or as the carpenter from Skoura said just after the May 2012 election had failed to produce a viable result: 'Just think of all those Skourai who sent their children off to be public sector workers; now this army of bureaucrats has proved to be Greece's undoing.'

CHAPTER 7

THE 'CRISIS' IN ATHENS

The last five chapters have focused on the provinces, the first two based on fieldwork carried out in the 1980s, the second two providing an overview of developments from the beginning of the 1990s to 2013. Neither type of village, astifiliac or agricultural, had been adversely affected economically by 2013 when I went to live in Athens for a year, though the town of Sparta was showing signs of pressure, such as an increasing number of shuttered shops. In the villages they said, 'We haven't been affected by the crisis yet (*then tohoume katalavi akoma* – we haven't understood it yet) whereas in Athens people are suffering.' It was Athens, characterised by economic stagnation and parasitism, which became the first casualty of the crisis, experiencing high unemployment, indebtedness and multiple business closures. This chapter focuses on Athens before and during the crisis years, its problematic progression from clientelism and tax evasion to bankruptcy and high unemployment, poverty and emigration.

The public sector

As a result of Athens' atypical development in the nineteenth century, the association between public sector work and a rise in social status evolved into an ideology that I have called *astifilia*. I have been exploring the relation between this phenomenon and Greece's long history of low productivity, arguing that *astifilia* has been a significant contributor to the twenty-first-century 'crisis'. As the historical accounts and most of the village ethnographies demonstrate, village life and agriculture were widely disparaged as backward, dirty and only for those too stupid to move away. When it came to twentieth-century returnees from abroad investing their savings in Greece, Athens was the town of choice, with real estate taking precedence over manufacturing or other forms of enterprise. At the same time as Pasok's policy of *apokentrosis* during the 1980s aimed to decentralise government services (when almost 45 per cent of the Greek population lived in greater Athens),[1] the state sector continued to expand despite government promises to their European creditors to cut down on handing out state jobs. By 2009 Athens had doubled in size over the preceding two decades and its population overwhelmingly consisted of state sector workers and numerous very small family-run businesses.[2] Much has been said about Greece's inflated public sector as a prime contributor to its economic problems. Some have responded that there are countries, for example in Scandinavia, with large public sectors that act to underpin the efficient functioning of those states. The points to bear in mind in relation to Greece are two: first, the *means* by which far too many citizens become civil servants, that is, non-meritocratically through clientelism; second, the nature of the bureaucracy in which public sector workers are embedded. This is such that even where there are competent workers the 'monster' state with its tangled *polinomia* – manifold (often contradictory) laws – obstructs the efficient expediting of business. A government history of combating unemployment by handing out public sector jobs, a very high rate of tax evasion, a large informal sector and endemic structural dysfunction in the legal domain have been major contributors to the economic crisis.

Debt

Given this background with nearly half the country's population based in greater Athens, a huge state sector and investors' preference for rentier income from real estate, it is no surprise that Athens was the first place to be seriously impacted when the global debt crisis hit Greece. Its parasitic economy and dearth of productive activity made it particularly vulnerable. In April 2009 when the debt crisis in Greece had only just begun to be recognised as such, Eurostat estimated Greece's debt to GDP at 115 per cent,[3] a sum subsequently found at the end of 2009 to have been an underestimate, with the actual figure 126.8 per cent.[4] A review of the economic changes over the two decades preceding the start of the crisis in 2009 illuminates some of the contributory factors. The 1980s was a period when around two-thirds of the population aspired to state sector work,[5] an aspiration largely realised as by 1992 one in six of the working population, or one in three of those employed in the tertiary sector, was a civil servant, a *dimosios ipallilos* (δημοσιος υπαλληλος).[6] Yet already in 1990 as we saw, the European Commission was demanding that Greece make a ten-per cent cut in public sector staffing by 1993, a cut entailing the loss of at least 65,000 jobs.[7] These measures closely resembled the troika 'crisis' reforms introduced 20 years later. The Commission's 1990 demands to increase revenues in order to ensure continuation of funding from the EEC's regional programme included the introduction of new taxes and new laws designed to reduce the enormously high level of tax evasion. But throughout the 1990s the country continued to run a budget deficit and in 1998, as noted, the EU judged that Greece did not meet the criteria for entry into the single currency because its public sector deficit was too big. However, echoing the 1980 debate and change of mind within the EEC, the European Commission subsequently voted to reverse this judgement. In 2000 it was decided that if the deficit could be reduced to an acceptable percentage of GDP, Greece could join the currency union in 2001. As in 1980, political calculations took precedence over well-founded economic scepticism. As we know now and many suspected then, the figures were illusory but politics prevailed.

Between 2001 and 2007, transfers from the EU triggered a period of economic growth and a consumer boom. Banks would telephone customers offering €1,000 loans in exchange for nothing more than an identity card. Loose lending conditions enabled a huge car-buying spree and the opening of numerous small businesses. Between 2000 and 2008, house prices doubled as people bought better homes and/or second homes. The colossal expenditure involved in staging the Olympic Games in 2004 hugely increased the debt, though at least it left Athens with an excellent transport system, which, unlike most of the sports venues, did not later fall into disrepair. The debt continued to rise as successive governments over the decade continued to tackle unemployment by creating more public sector jobs (thereby increasing their voter constituency) instead of encouraging more investment in manufacturing or industry. The 2008 Labour Force Survey records 1,018,000 workers in the public sector, 35 per cent of all wage earners.[8] In 2010, one in four citizens, almost 27 per cent of the workforce, still worked in the public sector, with more than 80 per cent of Greek public expenditure going on the wages, salaries and pensions of this workforce.[9]

Tax evasion

At the same time Greeks' aversion to paying their taxes continued unabated, as earlier-proposed administrative reforms to tackle the problem had lost momentum with the influx of EU loans at low interest rates. The level of tax evasion was exacerbated both by Greece's very large informal sector (estimated at 30–40 per cent) and the large number of self-employed (31.9 per cent versus the EU average of 15 per cent.),[10] many of whom were misreporting their incomes. A study of self-employed professionals (including accountants, dentists, lawyers, doctors) by the University of Chicago in 2009 found that under-reporting of incomes amounted to some €28 billion, or 31 per cent of the budget deficit. Particularly interesting is the light thrown by this study on who the prime offenders were. The researchers noted that in 2009 Parliament had proposed a bill requiring tax audits to be carried out on certain self-employed professionals including dentists, doctors, lawyers and engineers with a declared income of less than €20,000. MPs voted against the bill, raising the suspicion that as most of them came from these professions they would prefer to avoid scrutiny by tax inspectors. Furthermore, the researchers added, MPs may also have been acting in their role as government functionaries to protect powerful industry associations and guilds likewise reluctant to engage in tax reforms. On the basis of their findings the researchers judged that the principal tax evaders are the highly educated and powerful professions in Greece, that these professions are those held by the majority of Greek Members of Parliament and that they are governed by strong professional guilds. On average these tax evaders were estimated to be under-reporting their incomes by about €36,000 a year. In a carefully worded conclusion the researchers write:

> We document this association as suggestive of one possible reason tax evasion may persist. The alignment of the occupational backgrounds of Greek parliamentarians to our top tax-evading industries is *only an association*, but may suggest one possible reason behind the lack of willpower to enact tax reform. [My italics.][11]

Bailouts and the troika

In 2010 and again in 2011 the Greek government was forced to seek massive loans. The lenders, the European Central Bank, the European Commission and the IMF, known collectively as the troika, made the bailout conditional on the implementation of a detailed and extensive programme of austerity measures, fiscal and structural. These included tax increases, spending cuts, privatisation of state-controlled corporations, selling-off of state assets, slashing of salaries (though minimally in the case of MPs), reduction of pensions and the dismissal initially of 30,000 public sector workers, the first of 150,000 to be dismissed by 2016.[12] Already before the introduction of these reforms unemployment had begun to rise. Between 2009 and 2012 a quarter of all companies went out of business. In 2011, for example, 111,000 companies went bankrupt, 27 per cent up on 2010.[13] Jobs lost between 2008 and 2012 were in construction (188,000), manufacturing (175,000) and wholesale or retail trade and repair of motor vehicles (153,000).[14] To avoid a Greek default the troika agreed in November 2012 to a second bailout, with more austerity measures attached including a further cut to the healthcare system of €2 billion.[15]

The pace of change was frenetic and disturbing. Could sufficient thought have gone into the measures? Had there been sufficient time for the troika to analyse structural deficiencies before flooding the country with reforms? Neither the government nor the troika seemed to be getting implementation right. The Greek government's response was largely incompetent, sloppy and foot-dragging, more preoccupied with maintaining the perks of the privileged than addressing its corrupt and inefficient bureaucracy or corruption within its own ranks. If one wondered aloud why the troika had not insisted on lifting MPs' immunity from prosecution and substantially reducing their salaries, or, more radically, reducing the number of MPs (300 for a population of just over ten million), the reply came that this would be to exceed their remit. Yet the troika's intervention was actually very invasive – it was quite unclear where the boundaries between the powers of the troika and those of the Greek state lay. While it would seem reasonable for the creditors to demand reforms to promote transparency and cut wasteful spending in exchange for the loan of huge sums of money, it was not at all clear that the troika had sufficient grasp of the institutional dysfunctions and dynamics of state–society relations to enable it to dictate the most appropriate reforms and at such speed. Had it understood the probable effects on large swathes of the Greek population and concomitant impact on the economy? By 2013 the country had lost more than one-fourth (26.2 per cent) of its GDP, with a continuing loss in 2014. Over the same period Greeks' purchasing power had declined by 37.2 per cent and private consumption by 30 per cent.[16] Hardly unexpected in light of the job losses, pension cuts, tax increases and reduction of salaries, yet the troika were surprised that the reforms had not achieved the expected economic improvements. Their approach, strongly reminiscent of the shock therapy tactics imposed in Albania in the early 1990s by the IMF and the World Bank, threatened to end in tears.

The state

When a state ceases to provide reasonable public services such as in the health, education and social welfare sectors, when corruption is pervasive and bureaucracy impenetrable, obstructive or inefficient, when a state is unable to collect taxes or to address its debt, it loses credibility at home and abroad. In the autumn of 2013 Athens University was on strike for months at a time; students stood to lose the entire semester while the striking employees continued to draw their salaries. I was in a local shop where the strike was being discussed by a young man and the woman who owned the shop. 'It's a pity,' said the young man. 'It's a scandal,' I said joining in; 'twelve weeks and still striking! You might ask, is there no state?' I was invoking one of the commonest *cris de cœur* heard in chaotic post-communist Albania: *ska shtet* – there is no state. 'But it's precisely the state which is responsible!' exploded the shop owner. 'It is state employees who are refusing to work!'

Some months later while talking to a sociologist at a national research institution about the increasingly dire social and economic situation, I was reminded of this incident when she asserted that if anything is to be achieved it will be by circumventing the state and its mechanisms. 'They simply get in the way or obstruct; no help can be expected from them. None of us', she said, 'has any faith in the state.' Her assertion was backed up by a study Transparency International's Global Corruption Barometer made in 2013, which found that 90 per cent of surveyed Greek households considered political parties corrupt. Absence of faith in state institutions is a long-standing phenomenon in Greece and itself a big contributor to corruption. Why, it is argued, should I pay my taxes when I believe that our corrupt politicians will pocket my money? But if no one pays their taxes, one would counter, how can you expect to have state schools, hospitals and pothole-free roads? To which the reply would often be: the whole system is rotten; until laws are enforced for everybody, for big politicians and simple citizens alike, nothing will change. This is of course one of the core problems: the clientelist system encourages complicity in corruption at the same time as it confirms the colluding citizen's belief that the system is corrupt. Moreover the tangled nature of the bureaucracy, often opaque to the administrator as well as to the citizen, can often be sidestepped if the citizen can invoke the intervention of a local politician or, failing that, 'oil' (*ladonei*) the official either literally with a gift of olive oil or with another form of *miza* – backhander. The self-employed who under-report their incomes, and those working in the informal economy declaring nothing, are cheating the state of revenue. This then has to be raised by increasing the taxes of citizens who are either honest or whose income tax is automatically deducted at source from their wages (though even here there is scope for equivocation or working a second job informally). The manifest injustice breeds resentment, encourages deception and abuse and further undermines respect for the law.

Unemployment and pensions

At the beginning of 2014 the unemployment rate had reached 28 per cent for those over 25, and 61.4 per cent for those under 25. Even the large informal sector was said to have shrunk by as much as 50 per cent now that a fine of €10,000 was to be imposed on those caught employing undeclared labour. By January 2014, only 200,000 unemployed people were getting unemployment benefit, which like free healthcare is paid for one year only, while over a million had no support. 200,000 Greeks had moved abroad during the crisis, including many graduates and an estimated 35,000 Greek doctors now working in Germany.[17] Increasing numbers of students were joining the 50,000 already studying abroad. Most of the young people who stayed in Greece continued living with their parents; some remained jobless, some found jobs through family connections. Like many employees they often had to wait months before being paid. Their parents had in increasing numbers taken early retirement, worried that if they waited their pensions might be subject to further reductions.[18]

At the same time there turned out to be a surprising number of unfilled jobs. In a series of discussions on the crisis with a group of sociologists and economists in February 2014, I learnt that there were currently 400,000 unfilled job vacancies. 300,000 of these were low-paid jobs in sectors such as retail − 'jobs for low-qualified people', as one economist put it, 'that university graduates would not touch, as this kind of work is seen as demeaning or not worth the poor pay'. In this connection it occurred to me that the family was perhaps too desirable a refuge and educational status overvalued. Indisputably, however, the family in tandem with members' pensions has provided a vital safety net where unemployment is so high and social security funds virtually bankrupt. It was ironic when one considered the early age at which in previous decades a pension could be claimed − a big contributor to the country's debt − and the current situation where these pensions now support numerous family members including jobless offspring and grandchildren in addition to the pensioners themselves. As a taxi driver bemoaning the many hours he had to work to make ends meet concluded somewhat elliptically, 'Both my parents and my wife's parents have died.' It took me a moment to grasp the link between his long hours and their deaths – no parents, no pensions.

On the ground in Athens

The cuts to pensions had serious ramifications for most people. The first neighbour I met in the Athens apartment block I moved into in 2013 had just returned to live in the small flat she had inherited from her parents. She and her family could no longer afford to rent a large flat in one of the northern suburbs now that her pension had been reduced by more than a third. As for the formerly prosperous, one could find oneself in a neo-classical house with the cream of Greek artists' work on the walls and the owners at a loss as to how to make ends meet now that the breadwinner's pension had been almost halved. Sell a painting, one might callously suggest. 'Don't think we haven't tried. Who will buy them at more than token prices when so many other families are doing the same and the dealers know our plight?' Or in the words of another Athenian family trying to sell some of their property: 'In this climate we either get ripped off by real estate agents or fail to sell at all.' There was a view amongst well-off families who had prudently planned for the future that they were worse off than those who had always been poor. 'You see, it would be unthinkable for us to go to a *sissition* (soup kitchen) even though we are so short of cash, whereas for the poor it is not humiliating.' A questionable assumption and it was not just the rich who had sensibly planned their lives only to find themselves severely impoverished. The same problems affected every group of prudent planners equally unprepared for the shock of the crisis and the measures which came with it. As regards pride, I knew several struggling Albanian families who resisted going to the local *sissition* not because they could make ends meet but because pride forbade asking for handouts. They worked even longer hours in bakeries and shops rather than ask for help.

Amongst my middle-income acquaintances, strategies to make up for a fall in income varied widely from hiring out computing or translation skills, giving foreign language lessons, making and selling artistic bric-a-brac and providing dog grooming services, to giving up 'luxuries' such as buying new clothes, going out for coffee or having a cleaner. I heard two women on the metro discussing the reinstitution of patching clothes and darning socks. One family business close to bankruptcy due to the collapse of the construction industry (building activity since 2008 had dropped by 75 per cent, with a year-on-year decline of 20.7 per cent) took advantage of growing security fears and started making reinforced doors and window bars.

Property

One of the most striking early visual indicators of the crisis was the proliferation in Athens of 'to rent' and 'for sale' signs. Beside the road to the airport was an almost unbroken succession of these signs pasted on the fronts of commercial businesses. In the neighbour-hoods where I looked for a flat in 2013, 'for rent' or 'for sale' signs were plastered on every lamp post, telephone pole and available wall space. Many of the flats I looked at had been built in the 1960s, 1970s and 1980s, when returnees from abroad were channelling their savings into real estate. One reason for the frequently poor design was said to be the decision to cut costs by not using an architect. Frequently an apartment block had been illegally fitted into a space between other blocks so that a one-time view was now a blank wall or a direct view into another flat. Building regulations had been ignored with impunity or flouted with backhanders, *mizes*.

Speculative builders would often approach a plot owner with a deal (*antiparoxi*) whereby, in exchange for covering the building costs of an apartment block, ownership of a number of the apartments would go to the builder. Urban real estate had long been seen by returnees and better-off villagers as the best form of investment, producing a steady income for life and better security than a bank. Owning an apartment block in Athens conferred prestige and provided villagers' offspring with a dowry flat or base while studying, as well as rental income in an ever expanding city where tenants were easy to find.

But who could have foreseen the reintroduction of the *haratsi*? Amongst the new troika reforms was the introduction of a property tax, nicknamed *haratsi* after a hated form of poll tax imposed under the Ottoman administration. To prevent tax evasion this twenty-first-century *haratsi* was added to each property's electricity bill. It was calculated on the basis of a property's size, age and neighbourhood independently of the owner's income. Nor as each year passed was the tax adjusted to a property's current market value even though between 2008 and 2013 property values had fallen by 40 per cent.[19] Until 2015 it stayed at the 2007 'objective' price, the pre-crisis level. This was a killer for many middle-class families who often owned at least two flats or houses or even an entire apartment block. Almost all owned an *exohiko* (weekend house in the country) as well. Many landlords found themselves paying out more in taxes than they received in rents. As a result of the new measures including raised taxes, pension cuts and the *haratsi*, most citizens, landlords as well as tenants, experienced a serious drop in income. Tenants who lost their jobs either had to move out or ask for a lower rent. By 2014 far more landlords were lowering the rent than ejecting their tenants, a positive outcome for tenants which helped reduce social disruption. I visited a *symvolografos* (a notary specialising in real estate) who greeted me with the dramatic declaration, 'The property market is dead. No one can sell, no one can buy.

Those who own apartments rent at as low a price as will cover the tax; no one will be evicted because empty flats would cost the owner more.' Real estate transactions had fallen by over 90 per cent. Moreover, a new law, which would for the first time oblige the seller to pay a form of capital gains tax, was under discussion and no sales could be finalised until it had been passed. So the property market was literally frozen.

A number of radio channels devoted time to discussing those aspects of 'crisis' life which dominated citizens' daily experience. Day after day, month after month, the primary and often exclusive theme was economic: the debt; the loan; the spread; the yield; the 'real' economy. 'We are all economists now,' listeners and TV viewers commented wryly. It was frustrating when, as often happened, journalists and ministers talked or shouted through each other's comments, drowning out their points, but the programmes still provided insights into common preoccupations. Listeners were not following the broadcasts simply to wallow in economic misery, but rather to glean practical information on the latest reforms: where to pay your insurance; how to get free healthcare such as free vaccinations for your child; how to find out about the new non-brand-named and hence distrusted generic medicines; which new tax law under consideration might affect your budget. The broadcasts kept listeners updated as new laws were constantly being introduced, modified or reversed. One week a new law ruled that pharmacies' opening hours were to be extended – a welcome move – only to be reversed a few days later. When the odd scandal came up unrelated to the crisis, such as that of the allegedly misbegotten small Roma girl, one sensed the zest with which a change of topic from the usual worries was embraced in the media or between friends.

Inequality and *allilengii*

It was listening to these broadcasts that I first heard the word *allilengii* – solidarity – repeatedly invoked.[20] This struck me as novel in a country where *ta symferonda* – acting out of self-interest – was considered normal behaviour and regularly attributed to other people's actions. I had not yet found out the meaning of the word *allilengii* when I heard it used by a new acquaintance in an outlying northern suburb and asked what it meant. She put her arm round my shoulders to indicate solidarity. Later I asked her if the crisis was felt differently here from in villages. 'Villagers, pah, they're just fine,' she said visibly irritated: 'It's us town dwellers who are suffering!' So no urban–rural solidarity. I was still in the dark as to whom Greeks must feel solidary with or united solidarily against. Was it solidarity against the troika, solidarity between those now poorer, solidarity against those who had got away with embezzlement? Certainly in the autumn of 2013 people were united against a former minister of defence, Akis Tsohadzopoulos, jailed for submitting false income declarations and now on trial for receiving millions in bribes relating to foreign defence contracts.[21] The relish with which this trial was followed in the Greek media reminded me of the 1993 trial of Nexhmija Hoxha, wife of the Communist dictator, in Albania. Albanian television watchers hugely enjoyed the opportunity to condemn the luxuries in Nexhmija's house, luxuries they could not have dreamed of in all those years of impoverishment. Now in Greece Tsochadzopoulos' name was constantly invoked as a disgusting example of ill-gotten riches and corruption. Television reporters talked excitedly about *mizes mamouth* – mammoth bribes; demonisation of the wicked was a popular pastime. Yet a Tsochadzopoulos critic, parent of a poorly performing pupil, could unself-consciously talk of paying bribes to her child's teachers in exchange for better marks. The disconnect was endemic.

As I lived just below the Dionisios Areopagittou road where Tsochadzopoulos' house was, I found myself a participant in public censure. The first time I was asked by a Greek couple to point out Tsochadzopoulos' house I was mildly surprised but did not give it much thought. The sixth time I was asked I felt that the feelings aroused by the corrupt were feeding a social phenomenon. Then there were new developments: instead of gazing in wonder (or disgust) at the house, people started photographing it, the better one assumes to feed resentment when looking at the photo at home. Later on, people started taking pictures of themselves in front of the house. Did they now wish that they were the owners? Perhaps they did. One of the most visceral reactions to austerity measures was resentment at their unequal impact on citizens. Rich Greeks who had taken their money, ill-gotten or not, out of the country were escaping the effects of the reforms. Those least able to cope with falls in income, higher taxes, insecure employment or no work at all understandably raged against the injustice.

By 2013 unemployment had risen to 27.9 per cent, with youth unemployment at 58.8 per cent.[22] Though Greeks had lost 40 per cent of their purchasing power, food prices had yet to fall significantly. So it was not a surprise to find volunteers standing outside the neighbourhood's supermarkets on Saturday mornings asking shoppers to donate basic staples for local families unable to make ends meet. In a street halfway down to Syngrou Avenue there was a *Lesxhi* – social club, the centre where these volunteers distributed the donated groceries such as pasta, rice, oil, tinned tomatoes (and leftover bread donated by bakeries) to the families on their lists. One evening every two weeks families who were registered at the centre would arrive to collect their allotted rations. These families had been identified as in need by the heads of the primary schools attended by the younger children. It was members of the parent–teacher association who collected donations outside the shops and supplied the volunteers with the lists. I had approached the heads of some of these local schools after hearing on the radio that the shipping magnate Stavros Niarchos was funding a school lunch programme for the growing number of pupils in need. The primary school in my street was one of several institutions, from schools to community centres and charities, which I had approached. Contacting the head of this school had been difficult but I finally accosted her at the school gate and asked if I could make an appointment to see her in connection with my research on the crisis. She said I could telephone her. When we spoke she told me politely, 'No, we don't have any poor children; the crisis has not impacted on this school or on families with children who attend it.' I was given the same information by the head of another local primary school. With two exceptions every state organisation I approached (with or without a Greek friend from the area to vouch for me) was unable or unwilling to tell me anything about their work and whether it had been affected by the economic crisis. One woman who was the manager of a community day centre for the elderly said, 'Oh, if I were at home I could tell you lots but here I can't say anything.'

I was puzzled by this stonewalling; this was not a police state, after all, and even in Iran I had been able to talk to people in institutions about their work though they may have censored what they told me. Eventually a young lawyer friend clarified what lay behind these responses. Since the implementation of the troika reform programme to reduce numbers working in the state sector, employees lived in daily fear of losing their jobs. Saying nothing was much the safest policy now that these sought-after state sector jobs had suddenly ceased to be jobs for life. A new law by the Supreme Council for Civil Personnel Selection for the public sector (ASEP) regarding criteria for dismissal had been invoked and, as the visits described below indicate, it was not only those who had obtained jobs without taking the requisite exams or by presenting falsified documents who must go; everyone was now at risk of losing their job.

Public sector cuts

In February 2014 I learnt more about the cuts when a friend had to visit a social welfare (*Pronoia*) centre where she knew the director. Her errand was with a different official but she introduced me to the director so that I could ask about the centre's work. The austerity measures required, as noted above, a reduction in the number of public sector employees and the restructuring of government departments. One result at the centre had been the handing over of certain functions to the *Dimos*, the municipal authority, which the director said was now struggling to cope with the additional work. She added that whereas the social welfare centre operated on an impersonal level advising enquirers what steps to take, the *Dimos* acts 'personally' – *prosopika*; that is, getting help may depend on who you know – *gnorimies* – and what *meson* – connections – you may be able to invoke. Her own task now was to dismiss 15 per cent of the centre's staff, although, as she pointed out, dismissals would of course increase the welfare bills. She must grade each out of ten and dismiss those who were less competent. What evidence could she find to show that some were less competent? And how could she possibly do this, she asked, when they were all good? (A village shepherd's suggestion when we discussed this now common dilemma was: if they're all good retain the ones who would be worst hit by losing their job.) Another problem the director had was how to supply local schools with enough psychologists and health workers. The demand for these had risen enormously in the course of the crisis, she said, when families under the stress of unemployment or a fall in income were breaking up more. But of the sixty psychologists requested there were only funds for six and these six were so overstretched that their work had become more or less valueless. She now feared that the state welfare system was in danger of being completely dismantled along, she reflected gloomily, with the whole middle class. On a separate issue she was concerned that the hiring of cleaners, formerly public sector workers in these municipal offices, had been reassigned to private agencies that paid very badly and gave the cleaners no security. Might it be possible, she wondered, to form some kind of cleaners' cooperative?

Another official prepared to talk to me was the mayor of a *Dimos* in the north of Athens, introduced to me by a friend from the area. This *Dimos* consisted of seven separate *Dimoses* now merged into one. The mayor's office had lost 60 per cent of its income, so funds for each area of responsibility were severely limited; the *Dimos* had lost, for example, seven of its ten policemen. The depleted budget had to cover everything from road maintenance, rubbish collection, sports and cultural activities, to part of the cost of the *koinoniko pantopoleio*. This was a 'social' grocery store for the benefit of those worst hit by the crisis; its prices were subsidised and partly funded by sponsors from business, banks, foreign aid and the EU. It seemed, however, that the new austerity measures had not actually reduced local bureaucracy. There were 72 council members, and each project the mayor planned required the go-ahead of at least 35 other decision-makers. This meant, he claimed, that however pressing the proposed work, two years might elapse before an initiative could get off the ground. The rules concerning dismissals, as at the welfare centre, involved horizontal cuts irrespective of individuals' skills, productivity or experience; 15 per cent of the personnel must be lost. One mitigating development was that several retired individuals were now working on the council unpaid (though they had to be elected). We discussed the new administrative system named Kallikratis which had replaced the former Kapodistria system. Kallikratis aimed to reduce the size of the state by having fewer but more empowered (in terms of financial and decision-making powers) decentralised units and a reduction in local administrators. The buzz word was *autodoiikisi* – self-government – independence from central power. However, on closer examination increased centralisation looked the more likely end result as local administrators were to be under tight supervision from the Finance Ministry, to whom they must submit detailed monthly reports.

In 2012 on a visit to a town in the north of Greece (near Kozani) I had discussed the new Kallikratis system with members of the

Dimos there. Contrary to its purported aim of enabling autonomous decision-making away from central government, the members were finding that local initiatives, despite *Dimos* members' experience and knowledge of the area, were bypassed or overruled by central power. As the members put it: when funding is still under the aegis of the centre the priorities of the uninformed take precedence.

At village level, on the other hand, the removal of old-style village mayors – part of the reform – meant neglect as much as impositions. Initiatives for local improvements were not a priority for the town-based central authorities, and even practical issues from road repairs to problems with water supply took much longer to resolve. As Panayotis Karkatsoulis of the Athens School of Public Administration underlined in his lectures on *polinomia* and the monster state, 'For structural reforms one needs structures. But those structures tend to be complicated.'

Volunteers

In contrast to the beleaguered state sector workers, the women working at the *Lesxhi* distributing food had no inhibitions talking about their work as they were volunteers with nothing to lose. They may have had something to gain as they operated in a Syriza-owned building and doubtless supported the party, but their charitable activities were, I believe, apolitical. In the autumn of 2013 some of the families coming for help were from a neighbourhood school that had claimed to have no needy families. The volunteers said that of the 35–40 families coming for provisions about 60 per cent were foreign, 40 per cent Greek. Nine months later in June 2014 there was an increase in the number of Greeks and a decrease in the amount of donated goods. In Neos Cosmos, the neighbourhood immediately across Syngrou Avenue, the families had to be given cooked food as many could not afford fuel for cooking. On this side of Syngrou the nearer one got to the main road the greater the number of empty buildings and shuttered shops, and the dirtier and more pigeon-infested and dog-fouled were the streets.

The volunteers themselves were a very cheerful group of chain-smoking women, some retired, some themselves unemployed but with offspring or husbands in work. They were very nice to the families who came, asking after absent family members, well informed about their circumstances. The good relations were underlined one day when a young Moroccan woman came in with her children including a new-born baby. She had brought a box of cakes for the volunteers so that they could celebrate the new baby with her – they'd always been so good to her. By contrast, her reception at the hospital where she went to give birth had been far from welcoming: 'You've no insurance so you must pay double the normal fee.' (The normal fee was €600.) Neither she nor her husband had the required sum, but some relatives clubbed together and came up with the rest. Her experience highlighted two of the economic crisis' biggest casualties: the social security system, which had suffered a 40 per cent cut, and healthcare, which in 2012 had as we saw experienced a cut of €2 billion.

The cuts to the social security system, medicine and education proved the catalyst for volunteering, which had not played a significant role in Greece before the crisis. Traditionally the family has been the central mainstay for mutual support and stability, backed up by a state that provided generous welfare benefits (albeit far beyond its means). Community-based support groups have been the exception as the concept of civil society arguably fell between the stools of state and family. But as unemployment grew from 2009 and state institutions reduced spending, citizens' vulnerability increased, giving life to the notion of *allilengii*. Volunteering in the fields of social welfare, medicine and education has become much more common. In 2014 I heard on Skai radio that large numbers of tutors/crammers in Athens were offering their services free to the children of struggling parents.

Despite over-subscription to civil service and professional jobs and troika attempts to reduce the number of public sector employees, the aspiration for higher education remained undiminished. Parents were continuing to make sacrifices to send children to *frontistiria* or individual tutors after school, so help from these volunteers was welcomed.

Health

One of the recurrent messages on Skai's radio and television channels related to the philanthropic *oloi mazi boroume* (all together we can) initiative, which called, for instance, for citizens to come and plant trees on Athens mountainsides or, more surprisingly, to bring unused medicines to collection points around the city. It was astonishing to see on TV week after week, month after month, the sackloads, literally, of unused pills, bottles, ampules, being brought to the centres. Who prescribed all these medicines in quantities beyond their patients' needs? Popular opinion had it that doctors over-prescribed in order to make more money from the pharmaceutical companies. Whether true or not, widespread distrust on the public's part was unsurprising given their experience of many doctors' behaviour regarding payment. A patient might ask for a receipt and be refused point-blank. In a case involving surgery it would be usual to proffer a substantial unrecorded sum to the surgeon before the operation in addition to the final official fee, to ensure that they took greater care. A surgeon might demand a sweetener – the *fakelaki* mentioned earlier – if one was not spontaneously proffered. There was a slight risk that if proof of such a demand was presented to the authorities the doctor would be prosecuted, but instances of exposure are uncommon. A judge I knew whose mother had just had a knee operation paid a large sum to the surgeon beforehand. But you're an upholder of the law, I remonstrated. And she is my mother, he replied.

As regards the contributions to the Skai programme, it is true that Greeks are known to be overly fond of prescribed medicines, taking more than in most other European countries, but that such quantities could be dispensed with was surprising. If it indicated that many doctors were over-prescribing, it simultaneously highlighted the plight of increasing numbers of citizens without any access to health facilities. Between 2009 and 2012, spending on health had dropped by 25 per cent, with cuts in staff numbers and salaries and no prior detailed study to determine which measures could be taken without endangering public health. More than any other aspect of the austerity measures, the cuts to the public health budget emphasised the dangerous repercussions which occur when, as Stuckler and Basu observe in their book *The Body Economic*, those administering fiscal medicine are in denial about the cuts' effects. Their chapter on Greece entitled 'The Greek tragedy'[23] is an excoriating account of the Greek government's implementation of health cuts: the tragic effects the cuts have had on Greek citizens' welfare and the toxic combination of obfuscation and racism proffered in defence of the policies. For example, the authors report on the actions of Andreas Loverdos, minister of health in 2012, who was running for re-election just at the time when Athens' HIV epidemic had hit the headlines in the foreign press. Rather than addressing the epidemic by researching its causes and introducing measures to control it, the health minister chose to scapegoat a number of prostitutes, putting their pictures online, labelling them a menace to society and family morals, while at the same time axing HIV prevention programmes. Research by the Hellenic Centre for Disease Control was meanwhile discovering that the main cause of the epidemic was in fact the use of infected needles by drug users. Stuckler and Basu's urgent recommendation to the government at a conference in Athens in 2012 to expand their needle-exchange programme for drug users was rejected by the Ministry of Health on the basis that the drug users (despite concrete evidence to the contrary) were foreign immigrants.

In his first act at the end of June 2013, Adonis Georgiadis, the new minister of health (the fourth in a little more than a year), reintroduced a controversial law stipulating forced testing for infectious diseases under police supervision for drug users, prostitutes and immigrants – a move that is both unethical and counter-productive as it deters marginalised groups from seeking testing during HIV outbreaks.[24] The Joint United Nations Programme on HIV/AIDS called for the law to be repealed because it 'could serve to justify actions that violate human rights'. Since these radical cuts to the health budget, which so shocked Stuckler and Basu in 2012, the situation has further deteriorated, as this extract from an article written in July 2015 in the *Guardian* newspaper confirms:

> The Greek healthcare system is in meltdown after years of austerity. State-run hospitals have had to slash budgets by as much as 50 per cent in that time. Basic supplies such as gloves, syringes, gauze, cotton wool, catheters and paper towels have long been in low supply. The numbers of doctors and nurses is critically low. Rising poverty and rocketing unemployment have left 2.5 million Greeks – a quarter of the population – without national state healthcare coverage. (Health benefits are only available for up to a year after losing a job, after which patients must pay for their own treatment.) Screening for diseases such as uterus, breast and prostate cancers have been reduced, and with struggling patients unable to seek out primary care, patients are arriving for treatment at late stages when serious conditions have already taken hold.[25]

It should be noted, however, that a heroic effort to counter the effects of government cuts is being made by a number of doctors working selflessly on a voluntary basis in some city hospitals, part of a medical solidarity movement that is trying to keep healthcare afloat.

Conclusion

The ever-present threat of job loss for public sector workers and small business owners, unaffordable property taxes, high unemployment for many, particularly the young, successive cuts to pensions and the increasingly run-down nature of many areas where small businesses have closed down, are some of the depressing aspects of life Athenians have been experiencing since the crisis began. Many of the unemployed young people in towns living with their parents hope to eventually find a job or emigrate. Thousands of young professionals have already emigrated. Emigration is no longer only to western European countries; there has been a substantial haemorrhaging of businesses to Bulgaria, where not only are the taxes much lower but the bureaucracy is said to be quick and efficient. Some young families have moved back to their parents' homes in the provinces while a number have considered the possibility of returning to work in agricultural areas where their families own land. A government–EU programme offers training and some investment capital to people under 40 in exchange for a guarantee that they will work in agriculture for a certain number of years. But in 2014 few who looked carefully at the arithmetic took that step, fearing that their lack of skills and the size of the landholdings involved would not produce sufficient income to cover the needs of more family members.[26]

CHAPTER 8

BACK IN THE PROVINCES: DEPOPULATION VERSUS PRODUCTIVITY

In 2016, despite villagers' assertion that the few tourists who stay in the village are 'one-night tourists who move on once they've visited Old Mystras', outside entrepreneurs evidently saw things differently. Apart from one hotel which opened in 1964, there is an increasing number of new *ksenones* – guest houses – as well as a new hotel built by a local Mystriot and another very large hotel being built some way below the village by a wealthy Athenian. A successful restaurant, the initiative of a family from the neighbouring province, Arkadia, opened in the early 2000s. Its reputation for good food was deserved, and its business substantially increased by deals cut with tourist bus companies who bring groups to eat there after visiting Old Mystras. The family has continued to demonstrate proactive entrepreneurship, extending its restaurant and renovating two other buildings as guest houses.

Agriculture is not thriving. The fruit on the trees in the orange groves remains unpicked because this type of orange has been superseded by more commercially valued varieties and the juice factory is no longer sending pickers. One or two locals pick oranges from their groves for home consumption, but most of the fruit is left to rot on the ground. In the centre of the village in summer the smell of rotting oranges is noticeable and the trees themselves are growing too high. In some nearby areas of the province, locals are uprooting their orange trees, replacing them with olive trees or with new varieties of orange. Obviously this involves an investment of money and time before the trees are old enough to bring in an income. Given the predominance of very elderly villagers in Mystras it is unsurprising that such changes are not being made here. Mystriots' offspring living in Sparta could of course make such changes, but as the farmer said of his grandchildren, 'Not having been brought up to agriculture they would be unlikely to come to it now,' regardless of the 'crisis'. Unless the new tourism promoters can buck the trend, these signs of neglect together with the loss of population may symbolise Mystras' decline as a living village. But as a centre for tourism, albeit without indigenous Mystriots, it may take off. In 2017 the site of the Sassendas mansion, following several half-finished builds abandoned by different entrepreneurs thwarted by bureaucracy or lack of funds, is finally being turned into what may prove to be a euphoric retreat. The sign outside the site reads:

Euphoria retreat
Hotel & destination spa

The sign has an artist's impression of the finished complex, which looks imposing. The setting itself is attractive, semicircular on a slight rise with a background of forest. After so many false starts perhaps this venture will succeed. Another venture in Mystras, whose function is still a little unclear, is the Research Institute of Byzantine Culture. The website says that 'it was founded in 2007 in the framework of the University of the Peloponnese and functions in the context of the School of Humanities and Cultural Studies'.[1] Its main aims according to the website are:

1. To research aspects of Byzantine and Post-Byzantine History, Archaeology, Arts and Society. Additional emphasis is given to the study of the Peloponnese, particularly the area of Laconia.
2. To promote research at an international level and to facilitate affiliations with related centres and institutes.
3. To organize conferences and seminars on Byzantine culture.
4. To serve as an educational centre for graduate students from Greece and abroad. The Institute also supports the realization of doctoral theses.

The building that was the primary school (two of my children attended it for a year in the 1970s and another in the mid-1980s) is a handsome stone building, which took an extraordinarily long time between its inception as a Research Institute and its inauguration – 2007 to 2016. The building has always been closed when I have visited, and some sceptics have suggested that we might have to wait for the return of Konstantine Palaiologos, Byzantium's last reigning emperor, for a fully functioning centre.

Sparta for the first year or two of the crisis was cushioned from the impact by its location in the centre of an agricultural province. From 2012 onwards, however, more and more of its shops closed down until there were more shuttered shops than functioning ones. By 2017 the price of flats for sale had been decimated and rents correspondingly reduced. Returning to visit Voithia sto Spiti in 2017, I learnt that while the number of poor looking for help had not increased significantly, donations were fewer and smaller. Interestingly, the priest in charge told me that a number of those seeking help now came from poorer areas in the north in search of work on the land here in the south.

In contrast, villages like Mystras Kefala and the Parnon villages beyond had not been adversely affected by the crisis even by 2017, a positive trend noted in agriculturally active areas across Greece.[2] Productivity and incomes in the Parnon villages have risen continuously over the two-and-a-half decades since the end of the 1980s, a sign that low productivity is not an endemic national disease but rather one found in those areas where *astifilia* for historical reasons has predominated. These villages are also bucking the national trends socially and demographically. The young remain in the village, marry (later, in line with the rest of the country) and have on average two or three children, suggesting that these villagers feel comparatively secure as regards their economic future; nationally, the Greek birth rate is below replacement level. Approximately half the young couples are married to partners from within the village. Newly married couples live independently of their parents either in an independent unit above the parents or, more recently, in a newly built or renovated house of their own. Almost every household is connected to the internet, which is used widely by the young for educational purposes and by the middle-aged for news, entertainment and by some for shopping. A number of middle-aged villagers are well informed about economic and political affairs outside Greece; partly probably because Greece's economy is so closely tied to affairs outside the country, whether this concerns the debt and the bailouts or the refugee crisis. The Women's *Syllogos* (Society) has been active in recruiting teachers for different courses, including courses in cooking, in Greek dancing, and after-school English classes for the schoolchildren and anyone else who wants to join. The *Syllogos* also organises charitable activities such as the annual Women's Day supper, which raises money for NGOs such as Kivotos, the Athens-based multi-ethnic youth centre for children in need.

Kefala had, as related in Chapter 5, a flourishing cafe-restaurant joined to a shop owned and run by two brothers and their families. In 2016 a building owned by the *Dimos* came up for auction in the village's central square. The cafe-restaurant owner, unfazed by the national financial crisis, bid for the building and won the lease. Setting up the new restaurant involved considerable capital investment, an enormous number of bureaucratic hurdles and a lot of physical work reconstructing the disused building. But it is a sound move, as in the central square there is more space for customers, more space for their children to play, and better parking access for visitors from outside the village. The upper village restaurant has closed and will become a house for the second brother and his family. For the moment the grocery shop will stay open in winter but probably be closed in summer when it runs at a loss.

What distinguishes Parnonites' behaviour is their dynamic response to change, social and economic; their readiness to innovate, to experiment and to take risks. By contrast, astifiliac villagers have largely ignored both agricultural opportunities and alternative enterprises such as in tourism (agro or archaeological), preferring to move to public sector or service sector jobs in towns despite falling wages in these sectors. The consequence is usually stagnation and increasing depopulation. Where entrepreneurs from outside have come in with new initiatives might the jobs created draw back the young? Probably not, since these kinds of jobs (in hotels and restaurants) are usually done by family members or immigrants. More positively, in the case of one formerly depopulating village just off the highway going south from Sparta, 30 Albanian families have set down roots and are cultivating the land. This village is one of many in this area that like Mystras experienced high emigration. A man from Kefala commenting on people he knows in this area said, 'When I visit friends in these villages they could be from another planet. They don't talk about *horafia* (fields) or farming at all.'

The future

In 2014 the biggest change confronting farmers was the (long overdue) new taxation system, which required farmers to pay income tax of 13 per cent. Some villagers greeted the proposed changes with indignation and anger: 'They'll be taxing the stones in our fields next'; 'we'll have to sell up and work as slaves for the rich'; 'the young will leave farming as there'll be no profit in it'; 'how can we pay tax a year in advance when we can't foresee what next year's harvest will be worth?' In 2016 the government doubled farmers' income tax from 13 per cent to 26 per cent and increased it to 45 per cent on those whose annual income exceeds €40,000. The farmer is now required to maintain a bookkeeping system using 'receipt books' (*blokakia* – μπλοκακια) to be inspected every three months by an accountant. Social security contributions for farmers were also raised and a charge on water use, an irrigation levy, is planned for 2020. Inputs such as tractor fuel and electricity for agricultural use will no longer come at a reduced cost.[3]

I discussed farmers' likely response to these latest developments with an agronomist familiar with the village economies in this region. He believed that despite such high taxes villagers would in the long run be resilient. He did think that farmers would have to learn to cooperate as joint producers in collective schemes if they are to prosper in the future but, high taxes notwithstanding, concluded: 'The farmers in these agriculturally active villages have savings in the bank, pay what they owe on loans and take care of their money because they have earned it through their own hard work; they are not about to throw in the towel.' He might have added that in a country where unemployment is so high, alternative work would be very hard to come by. The fact that the statistics issued by the Ministry for Rural Development and Food show an increase in the number of young would-be farmers applying for start-up aid indicates the scarcity of openings in other sectors.[4] Perhaps there is even a growing recognition that agriculture has a future. In an interview in 2016[5] the Greek government's secretary-general of agricultural policy and management of European funds, Charalambos Kasimis, a professor of rural sociology, noted that the agricultural sector had been more resilient in the face of the crisis than other sectors: agriculture, forestry and fishery had been among the few sectors that boasted positive figures; its employment rate increased by 1.2 per cent in the years 2010–14, its added value by 6.0 per cent in 2015, while its exports had presented a consistent escalation since 2010, boosting the primary sector's contribution to the GDP by 0.9 per cent. Professor Kasimis added that over the past six years of deep economic crisis a timid yet steady trend seems to have been developing among Greek youth, who, in increasing numbers, have turned to agriculture to make their living. 'Indeed, there appears to be a tendency and an established interest to return to agriculture and rural areas,' he said.

Let us hope then that troika-mandated tax revenue targets do not result in killing off one of the few professions that is actually productive. It would be short-sighted of the government to overtax a group whose products make up one-third of the country's exports and account for one-fifth of all foreign income.

CONCLUSION

BACK FROM THE CLIFF EDGE

This book has examined some of the factors underlying modern Greece's problematic economic history. I have argued that Greece's atypical urban development in the nineteenth century and the role of a diaspora unwilling to industrialise laid the foundations for a parasitic economy and an ideology of urban aspiration. The country's geopolitical importance to foreign powers enabled this unproductive economy to survive unreformed (despite the repeated imposition of reforms). Behind the current bailouts lies a long history of serial debt, default and dependency. However, not every sector of the economy has reflected this stagnant image. The foregoing ethnographic history of two types of village, the astifiliac and the actively agricultural, illustrates how two different trajectories developed. Those remaining in villages where emigration had been high, the case for the majority in the 1950s, 1960s and 1970s, saw the future in state sector employment away from the village. In villages where emigration had been low (a minority), villagers exploited local pastoral and agricultural resources to the full. The image of farmers as backward and stupid persisted, while working in the public sector in a town continued to be associated with a rise in social status. But as radio journalists like to joke seven years into the crisis: there isn't money for us all to be public sector workers (*then iparhi hrimata na imaste oli dimosii ipallili* – Δεν υπαρχει χρηματα να ειμαστε ολοι δημοσιοι υπαλληλοι).

Clientelism (*pelatismos* – πελατισμος) has been a core contributor to Greece's huge debt. It has been the means by which governments recruited votes and the means by which job seekers obtained work in the state sector. High unemployment could always be combated by recruiting some more public sector workers. The ever expanding state administration and the concomitantly shrinking state coffers would become unsustainable and the trigger for foreign intervention, a loan and a regime of reforms.

I have highlighted low productivity as a major defect in Greece's economy. It is worth reflecting briefly on the differences between the astifiliac and the agricultural situations, the basis for my contention that *astifilia* has been a retrograde force while agriculturally active communities are open to change and receptive to new ideas. A public sector job offered financial security and social cachet but little opportunity for exercising initiative. Indeed, party political considerations favoured toeing the line. By contrast, a farmer whose income depends to a large degree on his own work and initiative is incentivised to try to maximise his gains by experimenting with new methods. Furthermore, he is not constrained by party political considerations when making decisions.

During the crisis, agriculturally active villages have done much better economically than towns. Together with tourism, agriculture is a positive contributor to the economy. On their own, however, these two sectors cannot bring prosperity to Greece given the massive size of the country's debt and the partial nature of some of the reforms. Nevertheless, in the eyes of the troika some progress has been made during the seven years of austerity as witness the headline on the European Stability Mechanism's website on 7 July 2017: 'ESM Board of Directors approves

€8.5 billion loan tranche to Greece'. ESM Managing Director Klaus Regling is quoted as saying:

> Today's decision by the ESM Board of Directors shows that Greece has completed the reforms required at this stage. The government and people of Greece deserve recognition for having come a long way in returning to fiscal sustainability and economic growth. The government should continue on this path to rebuild a competitive economy and regain investors' trust.[1]

May and June 2017 had been tense months for Greek government negotiators desperate to secure this loan to avoid default. Following the usual setbacks, stipulations and cliff-edge days of doubt[2] a deal was finally concluded and Greece received the next tranche of the third bailout fund just in time to avoid default. The agreement necessitated signing up to more stringent measures including further reduction of pensions and lowering the threshold for tax-free income. An impasse between the Eurozone members and the IMF regarding debt relief was temporarily overcome with an IMF statement that though they doubted the sustainability of the debt given its size and the conditions attached to the loan, they would contribute to debt relief 'in principle', meaning no actual funds till a future date. It was hoped that this 2017 agreement with the EU institutions would at last provide the certainty needed to attract investment to Greece and encourage the start of economic recovery.

The creditors and foreign auditors, meantime, keen to ensure that the required reforms did not lapse after the expiry of the third bailout program in 2018, were already considering what form of supervision could be introduced to keep the country on the straight-and-narrow thereafter. One proposal was to link debt relief to the implementation of reforms. A good idea in principle except that implementation does not guarantee reforms' ultimate efficacy. Take, for example, the new administrative system named Kallikratis, introduced in 2010. Its aim as discussed in Chapter 7 was to reduce the size of the state by having fewer but more financially empowered decentralised units (the unification of municipal authorities referred to in the passage quoted below). In June 2017 an article in the Greek daily *Ekathimerini* reported that:

> As many as 137 municipal authorities, which correspond to 42 per cent of all local authorities and 31 per cent of the country's population, have not published their ratified financial reports for 2015, according to a study by the Foundation for Economic and Industrial Review (IOBE) published on Tuesday. The report that analyzed the finances of municipal authorities also showed that 18 of them – i.e. 5.5 per cent of the total – don't even have any approved accounting statements for 2011, when local authorities were supposed to do so for the first time. The regions of the Ionian Islands (71 per cent), the Southern Aegean (68 per cent), Attica (53 per cent) and the Peloponnese (52 per cent) rank top among the 13 Greek regions with the highest rates of municipal authorities that have not issued their figures. IOBE president Takis Athanasopoulos explained on Tuesday that the publication of the local authorities' accounting reports is essential to scientifically assess the impact of the changes implemented in recent years with the unification of municipal authorities.[3]

Even without the missing reports I think we can draw some conclusions regarding the impact of this structural reform in Greece. The devolved response – doing things our way – to the Kallikratis programme of *autodoiikisi* (self-government) was not the one looked for by the reformers. Again, one recalls Panayotis Karkatsoulis from the Department of Administrative Reform:

'For structural reforms one needs structures. But those structures tend to be complicated.'

Efforts to reduce the shadow economy have had similarly mixed results. Some countries including Greece have introduced incentives such as tax rebates to encourage citizens to make payments electronically rather than in cash.[4] But actually preventing cash payments between citizens keen to declare as small an income as possible has proved very difficult. Consider, for instance, paying for a fridge or a television. The seller might suggest a lower price if you agree to pay cash without a receipt; or they may ask you to pay half the sum in cash and only half electronically so as to leave a smaller sum on the taxman's radar. Since paying in cash will cost the purchaser less the temptation is clear: both sides gain, only state coffers lose.

Another serious problem regarding taxes was highlighted in an article on the business page of *Ekathimerini* in May 2017.[5] It reports that the Independent Authority for Public Revenue considers only €11.4 billion of the €92 billion of taxpayer arrears can be collected and that this sum will mostly come from small debtors.

Consequently, the 0.1 per cent of debtors owing more than 1.5 million euros each have dropped off the IAPR radar. They are 5,551 taxpayers and corporations who account for 76 per cent of total debts to the tax authorities, or some 72 billion euros. There are even 69 state debtors who owe more than 100 million euros each that IAPR admits it is unlikely to collect. The tax collection mechanism is now focusing on the 2,388,899 taxpayers and corporations who owe a minimum of 500 euros each, who together make up more than half of all state debtors.

From these dire statistics it is clear that troika-appeasing measures circumvent elite groups (doctors, lawyers, accountants) as indicated by the Chicago researchers quoted in Chapter 7, targeting instead the less well-off or the less politically useful. This predisposition to exploit easier targets is now beginning to impact on the farmers – the producers. Farmers should be taxed, and were undertaxed for years, but as discussed in the previous chapter it would be very short-sighted if the government now *over*-taxes the one element of the population that is consistently productive. Obviously it is easier to impose taxes on tangible assets such as produce and fields than to police income from service sectors such as medicine, finance and law. So once again the elite evades austerity.

The persisting level of tax evasion and poorly performing tax collection raises questions as to the success of other institutional reforms introduced over the crisis years. For example, does clientelism play a lesser role today in the system than it did before the crisis? Are jobs obtainable through meritocratic means or are they obtained through connections, political influence or bribes? Is promotion at work achieved through performance or does it depend on party support or family connections? Is a bureaucrat's decision-making influenced more by political expediency than by moral or legal considerations; in a word, are bureaucrats usually *komatoskila* – party dogs?

On the subject of government dysfunctionality an editorial in *Ekathimerini* (8 July 2017) begins by highlighting the unions as an obstacle to reforms:

> Labor unions – and the government itself in no small measure – have been undermining, and with every means possible, any efforts at evaluating workers in the country's civil service.
>
> The union of public hospital employees, for example, has responded negatively to such efforts time and again in an attempt to hinder the re-examining of staff with degrees from 'suspect' private education institutes. Such incidents more than expose the pathetic condition of the Greek state

and its institutions. When you look at the mentalities and behaviour that have been holding this country back and have embarrassed it in front of the world for years, especially since the outbreak of the crisis, is it any wonder that reforms are taking so long?

The case of hospital workers is just one example, but when added to the many others in vital areas of the public administration, such as public education, we can see how difficult reforming the country really is.[6]

Bad management has undermined reform even when the right steps were taken. For instance, there were far too many civil servants, and their numbers were duly reduced, but thanks to poor planning some key branches of the public sector such as healthcare, the judiciary and tax offices (!) were left seriously understaffed. It seems that with respect to the troika's required reforms, successive Greek governments have prioritised austerity measures – increasing direct and indirect taxes, reducing pensions – over systemic institutional reform. Reforms to reduce clientelist activities or radically overhaul the bureaucracy have either been half-hearted or neglected. Moreover, those reforms which risk jeopardising the support of party members (whichever government is in power) have been avoided where possible. In a face-to-face society like Greece where nearly everything is negotiated through personal connections, from getting an old person a place in a state home to getting a job in a supermarket, it is unrealistic to expect overnight reform.

The most serious consequence of seven years of troika-led austerity is very high unemployment:[7] overall unemployment in March 2017 was 22.5 per cent (cf. Spain, next highest: 17.7 per cent), while youth unemployment in March 2017 was 46.6 per cent (cf. Spain, next highest: 38.6 per cent). Unsurprising then that Greece has seen a brain drain of the educated young, increased levels of poverty and, for some, despair. The extreme hardship faced in particular by town dwellers is evident. 'No other people would have put up with such a huge drop in income as we have during the crisis' is a not infrequent comment. It is true that despite the numerous strikes and protests many Greeks from a range of social backgrounds come across as more stoical than rebellious in the face of ever lower wages, shrinking pensions and increased taxes. Perhaps this is because they see that the hands of the government (whichever is in power) are tied by the European institutions. Moreover, certain aspects of Greek life are obviously helpful in the face of economic difficulties. First and foremost is the supportive nature of the family and the links that many town dwellers still have with their villages of origin where economic conditions are often better than in the towns. Less positive but not insignificant is the extent of the informal economy. The ability in Greece to live to some degree independently of the state mitigates hardship in times of crisis. Immigrants working in Greece used to joke that the Greek state may be bankrupt but the people are doing all right. Greeks say: where the state doesn't get involved things go OK (*opou then pleki to kratos ta pragmata pane kala* – οπου δεν πλεκει το κρατος τα πραγματα πανε καλα).

What can we conclude after seven years of crisis? Are the factors which I have highlighted as contributors to the economic crisis in abeyance? Clientelism has not yet been excised, though there is an increased awareness of its corrosive effect on government and trust in state institutions. *Astifilia*, the aspiration to work in the state sector, has to some extent been dampened by lower wages and fewer openings. But although public sector jobs with their sinecure image may have lost some of their social cachet, they remain a draw, not just because unemployment is so high but because, compared with, say, start-ups, they involve minimum initiative and fewer risks. The view that contact with the state is best avoided because it messes things up does not apply if it can give you a lifeline. Are farmers still seen as socially inferior? In the provinces a recognition, albeit slightly resentful, that farmers are prospering has begun to modify the perception that agriculture is just for the stupid; money talks.

Has the troika reform programme achieved any positive results to counterbalance austerity's impact of high unemployment and drastic cuts in social spending? Has the shock to daily lives galvanised the public into a rejection of state corruption and incompetence? Or do too many citizens still benefit from dysfunctional structures? We have seen multiple examples of the EU and earlier foreign powers denying Greek access to international clubs only to reverse the decision soon after. We have seen as many reform programmes imposing similar measures. Each time, the reforms fail to achieve their objective because the reformers never address the systemic flaws in the state administration or put an end to the lenient treatment of the elite (apart from the odd exemplary scapegoat). Imposing high taxes without tackling the monstrous level of tax evasion by the rich, or the disproportionate impact of austerity measures on the less well-off, is a recipe for revolt. If tax evaders continue to escape responsibility with impunity, public stoicism in the face of such gross injustice will turn to anger and crises of a different sort may emerge. These considerations together with the huge size of the debt to be repaid should make us cautious about looking to a speedy recovery. Nevertheless, the closing of this second review with Greece's creditors is a first step towards greater economic stability and one which will encourage investors. And whatever happens, Greece will continue to be one of the most beautiful countries in the world as regards its landscape, its inspiring antiquities and its rich cultural past.

NOTES

Introduction

1. W.H. MacNeill, *The Metamorphosis of Greece since World War II* (Oxford, 1978), p. 56; N. Todorov, *The Balkan City, 1400–1900* (Seattle, 1983), pp. 328–9.

2. 'To fund the independence war it waged against the Ottoman Empire from 1821 and to establish the new state, the provisional government of the Hellenic Republic contracted two loans from London, one in 1824 and the other in 1825. Bankers in London, by far the biggest financial centre in the world at the time, hastened to set up the loan, seeing it as a means of making a huge profit.' E. Toussaint, 'Newly independent Greece had an odious debt round her neck', part I of 'Greece and debt: two centuries of interference from creditors' (2016, adapted from T. Katsimardos). Available at http://www.contra-xreos.gr/ksenoglossa-arthra/1052-newly-independent-greece-had-an-odious-debt-round-her-neck.html.

3. C. Reinhart and C. Trebesch, 'The Pitfalls of External Dependence: Greece, 1829–2015' (Faculty Research Working Paper Series, Harvard Kennedy School, 2015).

4. *Financial Times*, 4 December 1990.

5. From Takis Katsimardos 'The Former Memorandum in the Greece of 1843', 18 September 2010 in the Greek financial daily, *Imerissia*, now discontinued. See also Dr Richard Dunley 'Echoes of the past: Greek debt and the International Finance Commission', National Archives blog, http://blog.nationalarchives.gov.uk/blog/tag/greece/ (2015).

Chapter 1   *Astifilia* and the Roots of the Greek Crisis

1. Cf. R. Dale, 'Learning to be ... what?: shaping education in "developing societies"', in H. Alavi and T. Shanin (eds), *Introduction to the Sociology of Developing Societies* (London, 1982), pp. 414–20.
2. Cf. B. Roberts, *Cities of Peasants* (London, 1978); A. Gilbert and G. Gugler, *Cities, Poverty and Development: Urbanization in the Third World* (Oxford, 1982).
3. 'The nature of the modern Greek state', in J. Koumoulides, *Greece in Transition* (London, 1977), p. 290.
4. N. Mouzelis, *Modern Greece: Facets of Underdevelopment* (London, 1978), p. 113.
5. 'Migration in Italy', in M. Kenny and D. Kertzer (eds), *Urban Life in Mediterranean Europe* (Urbana, Chicago, London, 1983), ch. 5.
6. Ibid., p. 187.
7. E. Friedl, 'Kinship, class and selective migration', in J. Peristiany (ed.), *Mediterranean Family Structures* (Cambridge, 1976), p. 364.
8. S. Silverman, *Three Bells of Civilisation* (New York and London, 1975), ch. 1.
9. Ibid., p. 227.
10. T. Crump, 'The context of European anthropology: the lesson from Italy', in J. Boissevain and J. Friedl (eds), *Beyond the Community: Social Process in Europe* (The Hague, 1975), p. 22.
11. Under Ottoman law all land belonged to God, but in practice ...
12. Viz. Mouzelis, *Modern Greece*, p. 77.
13. K. Vergopoulos, *To agrotiko zitima stin Ellada* (Athens, 1975); Mouzelis, *Modern Greece*; K. Tsoukalas, *Exartisi kai Anaparagogi O koinonikos rolos ton ekpaidevtikon mihanismon stin Ellada (1830–1922)* (Athens, 1987).
14. Mouzelis, *Modern Greece*, p. 106.
15. Tsoukalas, *Exartisi kai Anaparagogi*, p. 167.
16. Lefeuvre-Meaulle, cited in Tsoukalas, *Exartisi kai Anaparagogi*, p. 190, and Zolotas, cited ibid., pp. 228–9.
17. S. Gregoriadis, *Economic History of Modern Greece* (Athens, 1975), quoted in Mouzelis, *Modern Greece*, p. 164.
18. Quoted by Mouzelis, *Modern Greece*, p. 10.
19. P. Bickford-Smith, *Greece under King George* (London, 1893), cited in Tsoukalas, *Exartisi kai Anaparagogi*, p. 187.
20. Tsoukalas, *Exartisi kai Anaparagogi*, p. 204; K. Biris, 'La Société d'Athènes au temps du roi Georges I', *Hellenisme Contemporain* iv/2; Bickford-Smith, *Greece under King George*.
21. C. Cheston, *Greece in 1887* (London, 1887).
22. E. About, *La Grèce contémporaine* (Paris, 1897), p. 163.

23. Quoted in Tsoukalas, *Exartisi kai Anaparagogi*, p. 192.
24. A. Hamard, cited ibid., p. 211.
25. Bickford-Smith, *Greece under King George*.
26. W. Miller, *Greek Life in Town and Country*, 1905, cited in Tsoukalas, *Exartisi kai Anaparagogi*, p. 205.
27. J. Petropoulos, *Politics and Statecraft in the Kingdom of Greece 1833–1843* (Princeton, NJ, 1968).
28. Tsoukalas, *Exartisi kai Anaparagogi*, p. 230.
29. Ibid., p. 242.
30. Ibid., p. 253.
31. T. Stoianovich, 'The conquering Balkan orthodox merchant', *Journal of Economic History* xx (1960), pp. 234–313.
32. Tsoukalas, *Exartisi kai Anaparagogi*, pp. 292–4.
33. Ibid., p. 107.
34. Ibid., p. 110.
35. Ibid., p. 345.
36. Ibid., pp. 396, 505.
37. Bickford-Smith, *Greece under King George*.
38. Tsoukalas, *Exartisi kai Anaparagogi*, p. 398.
39. G. Finlay, *A History of Greece*, vol. 6 (Oxford, 1877), p. 16.
40. Cted in Tsoukalas, *Exartisi kai Anaparagogi*, p. 401.
41. Mouzelis, *Modern Greece*, p. 145; Tsoukalas, *Exartisi kai Anaparagogi*, pp. 486–8.
42. Tsoukalas, *Exartisi kai Anaparagogi*, pp. 407–13.
43. 1978:106 Mouzelis described this development as oligarchic parliamentarianism, as Keith Legg has noted in Koumoulides, *Greece in Transition*, pp. 283–96.
44. The phylloxera blight suffered by French currant growers in the 1880s had led to enormously increased Greek production in response to the increased French demand. But the French vineyards' recovery in the 1890s resulted in a crisis of overproduction for Greek growers.
45. Mouzelis, *Modern Greece*; C. Evelpidis, 'L'exode rurale en Grèce', in J. Peristiany, *Contributions to Mediterranean Society* (The Hague, 1968).
46. Mouzelis, pp. 148–9.
47. Tsoukalas, *Exartisi kai Anaparagogi*, pp. 150–7.

Chapter 2   Obstacles and Disincentives to Development in Mystras

1. W. McNeill, *The Metamorphosis of Greece since World War II* (Oxford, 1978), p. 106.

2. B. Kayser, 'Dynamics of regional integration in modern Greece', in M. Dimen and E. Friedl (eds), *Regional Variation in Modern Greece and Cyprus* (New York, 1976), p. 15.

3. *The Statesman's Year-Book 1990–91*, ed. J. Paxton, p. 571.

4. For example, P.S. Allen, *Social and Economic Change in a Depopulated Community in Southern Greece*, PhD dissertation, Brown University, 1973; J. Du Boulay, *Portrait of a Greek Mountain Village* (Oxford, 1974); M.J. Lineton, *Mina, Past and Present. Depopulation in a Village in Mani, Southern Greece*, Ph.D. thesis, University of Kent, 1971; S. Aschenbrenner, 'Reluctant farmers on a fertile land', in M. Dimen and E. Friedl (eds), *Regional Variation in Modern Greece and Cyprus* (New York, 1985), pp. 207–21.

5. Such as J. Dubisch, *The Open Community: Migration from a Greek Island Village*, Ph.D. dissertation, University of Chicago, 1972; M. Kenna, *A Study of Permanent and Temporary Island Migrants in Athens*, Report to SSRC on Project HR 2445/2 lodged in British Library; E. Friedl, 'Kinship, class and selective migration', in J. Peristiany (ed.), *Mediterranean Family Structures* (Cambridge, 1976).

6. Friedl, 'Kinship, class and selective migration', p. 364.

7. S. Aschenbrenner, *Life in a Changing Greek Village* (Dubuque, IA, 1986), p. 112.

8. Ibid., p. v.

9. Ibid., p. 119.

10. Ibid., p. 118.

11. Viz. E. Friedl, S. Aschenbrenner, N. Mouzelis, K. Legg.

12. Z. Georganta, *Draft National Report* (Athens, 1984); R. Lissak, *Urban and Regional Development, Democratic Planning and Evolution of the Five Year Plan for the Economic and Social Development of Greece, 1983–1987* (Athens, 1984).

13. A. Collard, 'The experience of civil war in the mountain villages of central Greece', in M. Sarafis and M. Eve (eds), *Background to Contemporary Greece* (London, 1990), p. 236.

14. D. Weinberg, *Peasant Wisdom* (Berkeley, CA, 1975); J. Cole and E. Wolf, *The Hidden Frontier* (New York and London, 1974).

15. Reining, C. (1980), 'The transformation of Hungarian villages', in P. Reining and B. Lenkerd (eds), *Village Viability in Contemporary Society*, AAAS Selected Symposium 34 (Boulder, CO, 1980); R. Andorka, and I. Harcsa, 'Changes in village society during the last ten years', *The New Hungarian Quarterly* xxiv/92 (1983), pp. 30–44;

16. W. Douglass, *Echelar and Murelaga* (London, 1975).

17. Weinberg, *Peasant Wisdom*.

18. K. Legg, *Politics in Modern Greece* (Stanford, CA, 1969), p. 105.

19. Karkatsoulis P. (2012), www.spiegel.de/international/europe/slow-progress-greece-struggles-to-make-necessary-reforms-a-809357.html. Many YouTube addresses including (2017) 'The Greek Reality of the Public Sector', on Greek Liberties Monitor https://www.youtube.com/watch?v=-W2zcfpeuiw.
20. In 2016 progress was being made by a new owner.
21. George Foster, American anthropologist, whose work includes studies of Mexican peasant society and social change.

Chapter 3   Social Relations in Mystras

1. Cf. T. Bottomore, M. Ginsberg and L. Coser, 'Social change', *British Journal of Sociology* ix/3, pp. 205–28.
2. J. Davis, 'The social relations of the production of history', iIn E. Tonkin, M. McDonald and M. Chapman (eds), *History and Ethnicity* (New York and London, 1989), pp. 105–106.
3. Cf. C. Lison-Tolosana, *Belmonte de los Caballeros* (Oxford 1966), p. 180.
4. Cf B. Shah, 'Problems of modernisation of education in India', in A. Desai, *Essays on Modernisation of Underdeveloped Societies* (Bombay, 1971, p. 247; R. Dale, 'Learning to be ... what?: Shaping education in "developing societies"', in H. Alavi and T. Shanin (eds), *Introduction to the Sociology of Developing Societies* (London, 1982), pp. 414–20.
5. Cf. J.S. Mill, *On Liberty* (London, 1874); G. Simmel, *On Individuality and Social Forms*, ed. D. Levine (Chicago and London, 1971).
6. D.D. Lee quoted in J. Davis, *People of the Mediterranean* (London, 1977), p. 71.
7. Some years later the café reopened but the gate remains closed.

Chapter 4   Kefala: Bucking the Trend

1. S. Aschenbrenner, *Life in a Changing Greek Village* (Dubuque, IA, 1985), p. v.
2. B. Panayotopoulos, *Plithismos kai Oikismoi tis Peloponnisou 13os–18os Aionas* (Athens, 1987).
3. Cf. J. Wagstaff, *The Development of Rural Settlements* (Amersham, 1982), p. 21.
4. Cf. E. Friedl, 'Lagging emulation in post-peasant society: a Greek case', in J. Peristiany (ed.), *Contributions to Mediterranean Sociology* (The Hague, 1968), pp. 93–106; S. Aschenbrenner, 'Reluctant farmers on a fertile land', in M. Dimen and E. Friedl (eds), *Regional Variation in Modern Greece and Cyprus* (New York, 1976), pp. 207–21.

5. Cf. I.T. Sanders, 'The nomadic peoples of northern Greece. Ethnic puzzle and cultural survival', *Social Forces*, pp. 124–6, quoted by J. Davis, *People of the Mediterranean* (London, 1977), p. 22.

6. The figures broke down as follows: 1 kg olive oil in 1990 cost 560 dr; a subsidy of 146 dr was paid by the EEC on every kg sold, bringing the farmer's income per kilo to 706 dr. From the income one had to subtract the 11 per cent of oil taken by the olive press owner for processing the olives, 440 kg in the case of 4 tons, plus the 250 kg consumed on average by the household. The EEC subsidy covered the costs of fertiliser, tractor petrol for ploughing and chemical sprays if necessary. Thus the farmer made a profit annually from his/her oil olive harvest alone, of 1,800,000 drachmae, not calculating his or his family's labour.

7. J. Chevalier, 'There is nothing simple about simple commodity production', *Journal of Peasant Studies* x/4 (1983), pp. 153–86.

8. Cf. Aschenbrenner, *Life in a Changing Greek Village*, p. 39.

9. A. Chayanov, *The Theory of Peasant Economy*, edited by D. Thorner et al., (Manchester, 1986).

Chapter 5   Social Relations in Kefala

1. S. Aschenbrenner, *Life in a Changing Greek Village* (Dubuque, IA, 1986), p. 50.
2. Ibid., p. 41.
3. Ibid., pp. 41–2.
4. J. Dubisch, *Gender and Power in Rural Greece* (Princeton, NJ, 1986), p. 51.
5. M. Herzfeld, *The Poetics of Manhood* (Princeton, NJ, 1985), pp. 65–6.
6. The Mystriot young men I questioned said it would be boring to marry girls they had known all their lives.
7. K. Legg, *Politics in Modern Greece* (Stanford, CA, 1969).
8. Cf. Aschenbrenner, *Life in a Changing Greek Village*, p. 74: 'The set of supporting families includes many, though not all, of the president's {mayor's} relatives, by whatever kind of kinship.'

Chapter 6   Provincial Changes from the 1990s: Stagnation versus Prosperity

1. *Financial Times*, 4 December 1990.
2. S. Aschenbrenner, *Life in a Changing Greek Village* (Dubuque, IA, 1986), p. 117.
3. The family who took it on are Mystriots in the sense that they have lived in the village for some years, but they came from Agriani. It is tempting to

suspect that it is not a coincidence that the majority of those who have shown initiative – the returnee who farmed, the young woman who married a Mystriot shepherd and set up a cafe-restaurant in the square and this family – are all Agriniates with no inhibitions about non-office work.

4. https://www.oliveoiltimes.com/olive-oil-basics/greeks-leading-olive-oil-guzzlers/35304.

Chapter 7 The 'Crisis' in Athens

1. P.C. Ioakimidis, 'The Europeanization of Greece: an overall assessment', in K. Featherstone and G. Kazamias (eds), *The Europeanization of Greece* (New York, 2001), p. 78.
2. P.E. Petrakis, *The Greek Economy and the Crisis* (New York, 2012) (96 per cent of Greek businesses had no more than four employees while 81.2 per cent had just one owner).
3. European Economy Occasional Paper 61, 'The Economic Adjustment Program for Greece', 6 April 2010. http://ec.europa.eu/economy_finance/publications/occasional_paper/2010/pdf/ocp61_en.pdf.
4. www.theguardian.com/business/2010/nov/15/greek-deficit-bigger-than-thought.
5. J. Manopoulos, *Greece's Odious Debt* (London, 2011), pp. 84–5.
6. Ioakimidis, 'The Europeanization of Greece', p. 77.
7. *Financial Times*, 1 December 1990.
8. http://adapt.it/adapt-indice-a-z/wp-content/uploads/2014/08/matsaganis_2012.pdf.
9. L. Papadimas and A. Koutantou, 'A Greek paradox: many elderly are broke despite costly pensions', http://uk.reuters.com/article/uk-eurozone-greece-pensions-idUKKBN0OW20W20150616.
10. www.ekathimerini.com/136072/article/ekathimerini/business/greece-tops-eu-list-for-self-employment-with-319-of-greeks-working-for-themselves. The European Union's statistical agency said that 31.9 per cent of Greeks are self-employed against an EU average of 15 per cent.
11. N.T. Artavanis, A. Morse and M. Tsoutsoura, 'Measuring Income Tax Evasion Using Bank Credit: Evidence from Greece'. Chicago Booth Research Paper No. 12–25; Fama-Miller Working Paper. https://papers.ssrn.com/sol3/papers.cfm?abstract_id=2109500 (25 September 2015).
12. www.ekathimerini.com/136945/article/ekathimerini/news/public-sector-overhaul-agreed, www.navigator-consulting.com/articles/public-sector-cutbacks-and-political-paralysis-in-greece/15, https://www.ft.com/content/d6314aec-ee72-11e0-a2ed-00144feab49a.

13. P. Hatzinikolaou, 'Dramatic drop in budget revenues', *Ekathimerini*, 7 February 2012; 'Pleitewelle rollt durch Südeuropa', *Sueddeutsche Zeitung*, 7 February 2012.

14. M. Matsagani, 'The Greek crisis: social impact and policy responses', Friedrich Ebert Stiftung, http://library.fes.de/pdf-files/id/10314.pdf.

15. D. Stuckler and S. Basu, *The Body Economic* (London, 2013), p. 92.

16. http://www.sidea.org/Benevento_14_files/KASIMIS%20-%20PREENTA TION.pdf. Charalambos Kasimis (kasimis@aua.gr), Agricultural University of Athens, Greece University of Sannio, 19–20 September 2014, Benevento.

17. *Guardian*, 20 January 2015.

18. This turned out to be a miscalculation as subsequent reforms did reduce the pensions of early retirees.

19. http://www.ekathimerini.com/203767/article/ekathimerini/business/greek-residential-property-price-slide-gains-pace-in-third-quarter.

20. I only discovered later that the government in 2011 had introduced a 'solidarity tax' to lessen the burden of the poor. Some found it ironic that this ostensibly charitable donation was not voluntary but compulsory. This was different from the moral–social solidarity being promoted on the radio. http://greece.greekreporter.com/2014/05/23/stournaras-wants-end-of-solidarity-tax-says-cheats-escape/.

21. An exception to a Member of Parliament's immunity can occur if the entire body of MPs is in agreement.

22. http://greece.greekreporter.com/2013/09/12/greek-unemployments-new-record-27-9/.

23. D.Stuckler & S.Basu, 'The Greek tragedy', in *The Body Economic: Why Austerity Kills* (London, 2013), pp. 77–94.

24. http://nsnbc.me/2014/02/21/suicide-hiv-infant-death-soar-post-crash-greece/.

25. www.theguardian.com/world/2015/jul/09/greek-debt-crisis-damage-healthcare-hospital-austerity.

26. Interestingly, statistics from the Ministry of Development and Food show that whereas there were 11,400 applicants for these subsidies in 2014, in 2017 there were 15,000 despite the now much higher taxes. More on this in Chapter 8.

Chapter 8   Back in the Provinces: Depopulation versus Productivity

1. http://ham.uop.gr/en/research/research-institute-of-byzantine-culture.

2. www.sidea.org/Benevento_14_files/KASIMIS%20-%20PRESENTATION. pdf. http://sustainablefoodtrust.org/articles/common-agricultural-policy-greece/.

3. www.aljazeera.com/indepth/features/2016/02/austerity-finally-hits-greek-farmers-160203061901398.html.

4. The government–EU programme referred to in Chapter 6, which offers training and some investment capital to people under 40 in exchange for a guarantee that they will work in agriculture for a certain number of years, saw a surprising rise in applicants despite these tax rises. Statistics from the Ministry of Development and Food show that whereas there were 11,400 applicants for young farmer subsidies in 2014, there were 15,000 in 2017. An indicator of high unemployment but also perhaps a changing attitude to farming.

5. http://news.xinhuanet.com/english/2016-12/19/c_135917262.htm.

6. www.sidea.org/Benevento_14_files/KASIMIS%20-%20PRESENTATION.pdf. Charalambos Kasimis (kasimis@aua.gr), Agricultural University of Athens, Greece University of Sannio, 19–20 September 2014, Benevento.

Conclusion   Back from the Cliff Edge

1. www.esm.europa.eu/press-releases/esm-board-directors-approves-%E2%82%AC85-billion-loan-tranche-greece.

2. www.ekathimerini.com/219841/article/ekathimerini/business/esm-tells-govt-to-do-its-homework-by-friday.

3. www.ekathimerini.com/219632/article/ekathimerini/business/tens-of-local-authorities-omit-figures.

4. http://iobe.gr/docs/research/en/RES_05_F_21102015_REP_EN.pdf.

5. www.ekathimerini.com/218668/article/ekathimerini/business/just-a-fraction-of-debts-to-state-may-be-paid.

6. www.ekathimerini.com/219900/opinion/ekathimerini/comment/the-enemies-of-reform.

7. http://ec.europa.eu/eurostat/statistics-explained/index.php/Unemployment_statistics, http://appsso.eurostat.ec.europa.eu/nui/show.do?dataset=une_rt_m&lang=en.

BIBLIOGRAPHY

About, E. (1897). *La Grèce contemporaine*, Paris: Hachette.

Alavi, H. and T. Shanin (eds) (1982). *Introduction to the Sociology of Developing Societies*, London: Macmillan.

Allen, P. (1973). *Social and Economic Change in a Depopulated Community in Southern Greece*, PhD dissertation, Brown University.

Andorka, R. and Harcsa I. (1983). 'Changes in village society during the last ten years', *The New Hungarian Quarterly* xxiv/92, pp. 30–44.

Artavanis, N.T., A. Morse and M. Tsoutsoura (2015). 'Measuring Income Tax Evasion Using Bank Credit: Evidence from Greece', 25 September 2015. Chicago Booth Research Paper No. 12–25; Fama-Miller Working Paper.

Aschenbrenner, S. (1976). 'Reluctant farmers on a fertile land', in M. Dimen and E. Friedl (eds), *Regional Variation in Modern Greece and Cyprus*, New York: New York Academy of Sciences, pp. 207–21.

—— (1986). *Life in a Changing Greek Village*, Dubuque, IA: Kendall Hunt.

Bickford-Smith, P. (1893). *Greece under King George*, London: Richard Bentley and Son.

Biris, K. (1950). 'La Société d'Athènes au temps du roi Georges I', *Hellénisme Contemporain* iv/2.

Bottomore, T. (1962). *Sociology*, London: Unwin Books.

Bottomore, T., M. Ginsberg and L. Coser, 'Social change', *British Journal of Sociology* ix/3, pp. 205–28.

Brewer, D. (2001). *The Flame of Freedom*, London: John Murray.

Chayanov, A. (1986). *The Theory of Peasant Economy*, edited by D. Thorner et al., Manchester: Manchester University Press.

Cheston, C. (1887). *Greece in 1887*, London: Effingham Wilson.

Chevalier, J. (1983). 'There is nothing simple about simple commodity production', *Journal of Peasant Studies* x/4, pp. 153–86.

Cole, J. and E. Wolf (1974). *The Hidden Frontier*, New York and London: Academic Press.

Collard, A. (1990). 'The experience of civil war in the mountain villages of central Greece', in M. Sarafis and M. Eve (eds), *Background to Contemporary Greece*, London: Merlin Press, pp. 223–54.

Coser, L. (1956). *The Functions of Social Conflict*, London: Routledge and Kegan Paul.

Crump, T. (1975). 'The context of European anthropology: The lesson from Italy', in J. Boissevain and J. Friedl (eds), *Beyond the Community: Social Process in Europe*, The Hague: Mouton, pp. 18–27.

Dakin, D. (1977). 'The formation of the Greek state: Political developments until 1923', in J. Koumoulides, *Greece in Transition*, London: Zeno, pp. 21–63.

Dale, R. (1982). 'Learning to be ... what? Shaping education in "developing societies"', in H. Alavi and T. Shanin (eds), *Introduction to the Sociology of Developing Societies*, London: Macmillan, pp. 21–63.

Davis, J. (1969). 'Town and country', *Anthropological Quarterly* xlii/3, pp. 171–85.

—— (1977). *People of the Mediterranean*, London: Routledge and Kegan Paul.

—— (1989). 'The social relations of the production of history', in E. Tonkin, M. McDonald and M. Chapman (eds), *History and Ethnicity*, ASA Monograph 27, New York and London: Routledge, pp. 105–20.

Dimen, M. and E. Friedl (eds) (1976). *Regional Variation in Modern Greece and Cyprus*, New York: The New York Academy of Sciences.

Douglass, W. (1975). *Echelar and Murelaga*, London: C. Hurst.

—— (1983). 'Migration in Italy', in M. Kenny and D. Kertzer (eds), *Urban Life in Mediterranean Europe*. Urbana, Chicago, London: University of Illinois Press, pp. 162–202.

Dubisch, J. (1972). *The Open Community: Migration from a Greek Island Village*, PhD dissertation, University of Chicago.

—— (1977). 'The city as a resource: Migration from a Greek island village', *Urban Anthropology* vi/1, pp. 65–82.

—— (1986). *Gender and Power in Rural Greece*, Princeton, NJ: Princeton University Press.

Du Boulay, J. (1979). *Portrait of a Greek Mountain Village*, Oxford: Oxford University Press.

—— (1983). 'The meaning of dowry: Changing values in rural Greece', *Journal of Modern Greek Studies* i/2, pp. 243–70.

Du Boulay, J. and R. Williams (1987). 'Amoral familism and the image of limited good', *Anthropological Quarterly* lx/1, pp. 12–24.

Dunley, R. (2015). 'Echoes of the past: Greek debt and the International Finance Commission', National Archives blog, http://blog.nationalarchives.gov.uk/blog/tag/greece/.

Evelpidis, C. (1968). 'L'exode rurale en Grèce', in J. Peristiany, *Contributions to Mediterranean Society*, The Hague: Mouton, pp. 127–40.

Featherstone K. and G. Kazamias (eds) (2001). *The Europeanization of Greece*, New York: Frank Cass & Co.

Finlay, G. (1877). *A History of Greece*, vols 4–7, Oxford: Clarendon Press.

Foster, G. (1965). 'Peasant society and the image of limited good', *American Anthropologist* lxvii/2, pp. 293–315.

Friedl, E. (1962). *Vasilika*, New York: Holt, Rinehart and Winston.

—— (1968). 'Lagging emulation in post-peasant society: a Greek case', in J. Peristiany (ed.), *Contributions to Mediterranean Sociology*, The Hague: Mouton, pp. 93–106.

—— (1976). 'Kinship, class and selective migration', in J. Peristiany (ed.), *Mediterranean Family Structures*, Cambridge: Cambridge University Press.

—— (1986). 'The position of women: appearance and reality', in J. Dubisch, *Gender and Power in Rural Greece*, Princeton, NJ: Princeton University Press.

Georganta, Z. (1984). *Draft National Report*, Athens: KEPE (Centre of Economic Research).

Gilbert, A. and G. Gugler (1982). *Cities, Poverty and Development: Urbanization in the Third World*, Oxford: Oxford University Press.

Ginsberg, M. (1958). 'Social change', *British Journal of Sociology* ix/3, pp. 205–28.

Gregoriadis, S. (1975). *Economic History of Modern Greece*, Athens: Polaris (in Greek).

Hamard, Abbé (1890). *Par dela l'Adriatique et les Balkans*, Paris: Delhomme et Briguet.

Hatzinokolaou, P. (2012). 'Dramatic drop in budget revenues', *Ekathimerini*, 7 February 2012; 'Pleitewelle rollt durch Südeuropa', *Sueddeutsche Zeitung*, 7 February 2012.

Herzfeld, M. (1984). 'The horns of the Mediterraneanist dilemma', *American Ethnologist* 11, pp. 439–54.

—— (1985). *The Poetics of Manhood*, Princeton, NJ: Princeton University Press.

—— (1987). *Anthropology through the Looking-Glass*, Cambridge: Cambridge University Press.

Ioakimidis, P.C. (2001). 'The Europeanization of Greece: An overall assessment', in K. Featherstone and G. Kazamias (eds), *The Europeanization of Greece*, New York: Frank Cass & Co.

Jacobides, M.G. 'Public Administration and the Tragic Trident: Understanding the Organizational and Structural Drivers of the Greek Malaise', London Business School, In Meghir, C., Pissarides, C., Vayanos, D., Vettas, N. (eds), *The Greek Economy*, MIT Press, forthcoming 2017 www.pbc.gr/btb/Breaking_the_bottlenecks_Jacobides_paper.pdf.

Karantinos, D. (2013). 'The Social and Employment Situation in Greece', National Centre for Social Research EKKE Athens, www.europarl. europa.eu/RegData/etudes/note/join/2013/507491/IPOL-EMPL_NT(2013) 507491_EN.pdf.

Karantinos, D. (2014). 'An evaluation of the social and employment aspects and challenges in Greece'. Employment and Social Affairs Committee homepage at www.europarl.europa.eu/EMPL. Manuscript completed in January 2014.

Karkatsoulis, P. (2017). 'The Greek Reality of the Public Sector', address on YouTube Greek Liberties Monitor, www.youtube.com/watch?v= W2zcfpeuiw.

Kasimis, C. (2014). 'The economic crisis and return to the land in Greece: What lessons for rural development policies?' Agricultural University of Athens, Greece Conference paper given at University of Sannio 19–20 September 2014, Benevento, www.sidea.org/Benevento_14_files/KASIMIS%20-% 20PRESENTATION.pdf.

Kayser, B. (1976). 'Dynamics of regional integration in modern Greece', in M. Dimen and E. Friedl (eds), *Regional Variation in Modern Greece and Cyprus*, New York: The New York Academy of Sciences.

Kenna, M. (1974). *A Study of Permanent and Temporary Island Migrants in Athens*, Report to Social Sciences Research Councilon Project HR 2445/2 lodged in British Library.

Kenny, M. and D. Kertzer (eds) (1983). *Urban Life in Mediterranean Europe*, Urbana, London: University of Illinois.

Knight, D.M. (2015). *History, Time and Economic Crisis in Central Greece*, London: Palgrave.

Koumoulides, J. (ed.) (1977). *Greece in Transition*, London: Zeno.

Lapavitsas, C. (2013). *Profiting without Producing*, London: Verso.

Lefeuvre-Meaulle, H. (1916). *La Grèce economique et financière en 1915*, Paris: FelixAlcan.

Legg, K. (1969). *Politics in Modern Greece*, Stanford, CA: Stanford University Press.

—— (1977). 'The nature of the modern Greek state', in J. Koumoulides (ed.), *Greece in Transition*, London: Zeno, pp. 283–96.

Lineton, M. (1971). *Mina, Past and Present. Depopulation in a Village in Mani, Southern Greece*, PhD thesis, University of Kent.

Lison-Tolosana, C. (1966). *Belmonte de los Caballeros*, Oxford: Clarendon Press.

Lissak, R. (1984). *Urban and Regional Development, Democratic Planning and Evolution of the Five Year Plan for the Economic and Social Development of Greece, 1983–1987*, Athens: KEPE (Centre of Economic Research).

Manolopoulos, J. (2011). *Greece's Odious Debt*, London: Anthem Press.

Matsagani, M. (2013). 'The Greek crisis: social impact and policy responses', Friedrich Ebert Stiftung, http://library.fes.de/pdf-files/id/10314.pdf.

McGrew, W. (1985). *Land and Revolution in Modern Greece 1800–1881*, Kent, OH: The Kent State University Press.

McNeill, W. (1978). *The Metamorphosis of Greece since World War II*, Oxford: Basil Blackwell.

Mill, J.S. (1874). *On Liberty*, London: Longmans, Green, Reader, Dyer.

Miller, W. (1905). *Greek Life in Town and Country*, London: George Newnes.

Mouzelis, N. (1978). *Modern Greece: Facets of Underdevelopment*, London: Macmillan.

—— (1979). 'Peasant agriculture, productivity and the laws of capitalist development: A reply to Vergopoulos', *Journal of Peasant Studies* vi/3, pp. 351–7.

BIBLIOGRAPHY

—— (1986). *Politics in the Semi-Periphery; Early Parliamentarism and Late Industrialisation in the Balkans and Latin America*, Basingstoke: Macmillan.

Palaiologos, Y. (2014). *13th Labour of Hercules*, London: Portobello Books Ltd.

Panayotopoulos, B. (1987). *Plithismos kai Oikismoi tis Peloponnisou 13os–18os Aionas* (Population and Settlements in the Peloponnese 13th–18th Centuries), Athens: Istoriko Arheio Emboriki Trapeza tis Ellados.

Papadimas, L. and A. Koutantou (2015). 'A Greek paradox: many elderly are broke despite costly pensions', http://uk.reuters.com/article/uk-eurozone-greece-pensions-idUKKBN0OW20W20150616.

Peristiany, J. (ed.) (1968). *Contributions to Mediterranean Sociology*, The Hague: Mouton.

—— (ed.) (1976). *Mediterranean Family Structures*, Cambridge: Cambridge University Press.

Petrakis, P.E. (2012). *The Greek Economy and the Crisis*, New York: Springer.

Petropoulos, J. (1968). *Politics and Statecraft in the Kingdom of Greece 1833–1843*, Princeton, NJ: Princeton University Press.

Price, V. (2013). *Greekonomics*, London: Biteback Publishing.

Reinhart, C. and C. Trebesch (2015). 'The Pitfalls of External Dependence: Greece, 1829–2015', Faculty Research Working Paper Series Harvard Kennedy School.

Reining, C. (1980). 'The transformation of Hungarian villages', in P. Reining and B. Lenkerd (eds), *Village Viability in Contemporary Society*, AAAS Selected Symposium 34, Boulder, CO: Westview Press, pp. 109–12.

Reining, P. and B. Lenkerd (eds) (1980). *Village Viability in Contemporary Society*, AAAS Selected Symposium 34, Boulder, CO: Westview Press.

Roberts, B. (1978). *Cities of Peasants*, London: Edward Arnold.

Sanders, I. (1954). 'The nomadic peoples of northern Greece. Ethnic puzzle and cultural survival', *Social Forces* xxxiii, pp. 122–9.

Sarafis, M. and M. Eve (eds) (1990). *Background to Contemporary Greece*, London: Merlin Press.

Shah, B. (1971). 'Problems of modernisation of education in India', in A. Desai, *Essays on Modernisation of Underdeveloped Societies*, Bombay: Thacker, pp. 240–53.

Shanin, T. (1988). *Defining Peasants*, Oxford: Basil Blackwell.

Silverman, S. (1975). *Three Bells of Civilisation*, New York and London: Columbia University Press.

Simmel, G. (1971). *On Individuality and Social Forms* (ed. D. Levine), Chicago and London: University of Chicago Press.

Smith, C. (1984). 'Forms of production in practice: Fresh approaches to simple commodity production', *Journal of Peasant Studies* xi/4, pp. 201–21.

Stoianovich, T. (1960). 'The conquering Balkan Orthodox merchant', *Journal of Economic History* xx, pp. 234–313.

Stuckler, D. and S. Basu (2013). *The Body Economic: Why Austerity Kills*, London, Allen Lane.

Bibliography

Todorov, N. (1983). *The Balkan City, 1400–1900*, Seattle: University of Washington Press.

Toussaint, E. (2016). 'Newly independent Greece had an odious debt round her neck', part I of the series 'Greece and debt: Two centuries of interference from creditors' (adapted from Takis Katsimardos). Available at www.cadtm.org/Newly-Independent-Greece-had-an#nh2-11, www.contra-xreos.gr/ksenoglossa-arthra/1052-newly-independent-greece-had-an-odious-debt-round-her-neck.html.

Tsoukalas, K. (1976). 'Some aspects of "over-education" in modern Greece', in M. Dimen, and E. Friedl, *Regional Variation in Modern Greece and Cyprus*, New York: The New York Academy of Sciences, pp. 419–28.

—— (1987). *Exartisi kai Anaparagogi O koinonikos rolos ton ekpaidevtikon mihanismon stin Ellada (1830–1922)* (Dependence and Reproduction. The Social Role of the Educational Mechanism in Greece), Athens: Themelio.

Tziovas D. (ed.) (2009). *Greek Diaspora and Migration since 1700*, Oxford: Taylor & Francis.

Vergopoulos, K. (1975). *To agrotiko zitima stin Ellada* (The Agricultural Issue in Greece), Athens: Exantas.

—— (1978). 'Capitalism and peasant productivity', *Journal of Peasant Studies* v/4, pp. 446–65.

Wagstaff, J. (1982). *The Development of Rural Settlements*, Amersham: Avebury.

Weinberg, D. (1975). *Peasant Wisdom*, Berkeley: University of California Press.

INDEX